The Making of Captains of Lives

Prison Reform in Singapore:
1999 to 2007

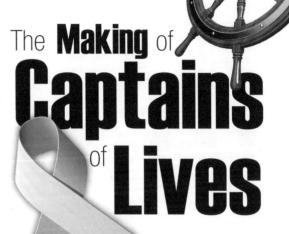

The **Making** of **Captains** of **Lives**

Prison Reform in Singapore:
1999 to 2007

Chua Chin Kiat

Centre For Enabled Living, Singapore

World Scientific

NEW JERSEY • LONDON • SINGAPORE • BEIJING • SHANGHAI • HONG KONG • TAIPEI • CHENNAI

Published by

World Scientific Publishing Co. Pte. Ltd.

5 Toh Tuck Link, Singapore 596224

USA office: 27 Warren Street, Suite 401-402, Hackensack, NJ 07601

UK office: 57 Shelton Street, Covent Garden, London WC2H 9HE

Library of Congress Cataloging-in-Publication Data
Chua, Chin Kiat.
   The making of captains of lives : prison reform in Singapore, 1999 to 2007 / Chua Chin Kiat.
    p. cm.
  Includes bibliographical references.
   ISBN 978-9814383820 -- ISBN 9814383821
   1. Prisons--Singapore. 2. Criminals--Rehabilitation--Singapore. 3. Prisoners--Singapore.
I. Title.
  HV9800.67.C46 2012
  365'.7095957090511--dc23

                   2012002827

British Library Cataloguing-in-Publication Data
A catalogue record for this book is available from the British Library.

In-house Editor: Lum Pui Yee

Typeset by Stallion Press
Email: enquiries@stallionpress.com

Printed in Singapore by Mainland Press Pte Ltd.

This book tells a story of successful prison reform that brought the recidivism rate of prisoners down from 44% to 24%. In the process of this reform, the entire Prison Service was transformed from a custody focused mindset to a rehabilitation centred culture. This change was wrought despite the lack of enthusiasm of the then political leadership.

The author describes his personal role in the reform effort, the methodology used to engender change in organisational culture and the struggles for the soul of the prison service, and the hearts and minds of all those involved. These include organisations involved in the aftercare of ex-offenders, volunteers who came forward to assist, and the families and employers of offenders and ex-offenders. The journey ends with the Yellow Ribbon Project that now embodies the rehabilitative efforts for ex-offenders.

The Making of Captains of Lives is a personal account of a public sector leader who has helped built a highly efficient prison system in Singapore, providing a strong case study for successful change management and public sector leadership. It will encourage the hearts of all those civil servants who believe in serving their nations and societies by devoting themselves to a worthy cause in their day-to-day work.

PREFACE

The Making of the Captains of Lives

Reflections by Professor Thomas Hellwig, INSEAD Global Leadership Center

Let me start with the biggest surprise to me: The "Captains of Lives" story also changed my life.

"Looking for the sparkle not just the flaw in every individual" is a powerful message of the prison officers of Singapore with an impact beyond the walls of prison. My opinion prior to hearing about the "Captains of Lives" was mainly shaped by books, newspapers and movies. Gaining access to all people from the Director of prison to long-serving inmates allowed me to really experience and evaluate this incredible story. It changed my views about prisons, inmates, prison guards and the way society organise its correctional service.

"Giving people a second chance" is the motto of the "Yellow Ribbon Project." This is at the same time the key message I took away from this transformation journey into my work as a professor of leadership at INSEAD, one of the top business schools of the world.

I might also share an anecdote of two executives who came to see me two days after the class in a program at INSEAD. After further reflections they claimed that they came to the conclusion that the motto *"Give people a second chance"* is equally important to teams and organisations in the business world. According to them there is the tendency in many companies only to give employees a single chance. This fear of failure could paralyse people and perhaps keep them away from achieving their full potential. This insight reminded me indeed of a reflection that Mr Chua shared with me in one of our conversations: *faith energizes, fear paralyses*. Again and again, I am positively surprised by the reactions that this story provokes among executives beyond the walls of prison and even its importance for leaders beyond the public service.

The book *"The Making of the Captains of Lives"* is more than a modern fairytale of a successful organisational change. It is the true story of an amazing project of the transformation of an organisation where most people would least expect to find examples of inspirational leadership and business excellence: The Singapore Prison Service. This story started out of necessity (overcrowded prisons, lack of motivated staff and ageing facilities), involved the whole organisation and eventually changed the mindset of those who started the process and many other Singaporeans. Giving people a second chance is a credo that generated change dynamics beyond the prison walls: the "Captains of Lives" continue to affect how Singaporeans view prisons and prisoners.

As professors of INSEAD, one of the top-tier business schools in the world, we are constantly looking for unusual examples of authentic leadership and organisational change from which senior international executives can learn. At the INSEAD Global Leadership Center, the well-known business professor Manfred R Kets de Vries and I got interested in this story in 2007 when Mr Chua Chin Kiat attended a management program at INSEAD. As he happened to undergo one of the leadership modules run by our Center, I worked closely with him and learned about the "Captains of Lives" story. My initial reaction was rather skeptical. Very often, the stories managers and leaders claim to have experienced are in reality not as impressive as they seem.

However, when meeting Mr Chua Chin Kiat for the first time in person, I realized that he was different. I experienced a very sharp, analytical, confident and determined but also mindful, curious and self-reflective leader. Although we had an intensive interaction during the program, we only started talking about the idea of collaboration after the course had ended. As Mr Chua concluded his appointment as the Director of the Singapore Prison Service (SPS), the idea of writing a book about the whole story was already well established in his mind. His main audience was public servants especially in Asia. He wanted to share his experience, having undertaken a change journey in a public service. Although I found this concept very well targeted from the beginning, I was convinced that many of the insights Mr Chua and his team gained throughout the organisational transformation, were hugely interesting to an even wider audience of business and public leaders around the world. After further discussion, we decided to start collaborating in order to write a business case for INSEAD. To do so we had to overcome skeptics on both sides. After Mr Chua retired from his post as Director of SPS in 2007, it was the decision of his successor to evaluate the benefits of a partnership with a business school. As in most public services around the world, security concerns got in the way when dealing with highly confidential data. However, it also took some persuasion to find support within the business academia: Who would be interested to read about prisons? What can we really learn from such a story? It is enough to read the stories about prisons in Western countries to understand that this is not an environment where we can expect to find something of interest. Why should that be different in Singapore? Nevertheless, due to the persistence and determination on both sides, we not only published the INSEAD case study and use it regularly in executive education but Mr Chua also brought this book to publication.

INSEAD and the Global Leadership Center are grateful to Mr Chua, the Singapore Prison Service and the Ministry of Home Affairs for their cooperation. We support this book thoroughly as it gives a real example of transformational change of an organisation triggered by sheer necessity, supported by an inspired leadership team. The change of paradigm has affected the mindset of an entire society.

Reflections of "The Making of the Captains of Lives"

When reflecting on "The Making of the Captains of Lives" we could take many different perspectives. Is this a pure story about inspirational leadership or organisational change? Is the collective aspect of the change of culture more important or the effect on the collective mindset of Singaporeans? Perhaps one could even apply a very simplistic approach: when a public manager or leader is faced with an extremely difficult situation, great things can be achieved; when the clear analysis is followed by dedicated collective action. Leadership is not something given at birth but has to be developed again and again when faced with mountains that seem too high to climb.

As in many things in life, the longer we look and experience it, the more we appreciate the different aspects of the story and gain further value from it. Through my interactions with Mr Chua over the years, I learned that the Captains of Lives story changed not only his mindset and understanding of the prison system but also that of many others involved with it. When approaching the story initially, I had a different understanding of it than I have today. Looking with the eyes of a Western leadership academic, I thought in the beginning that this is a true story of inspirational leadership of a man on a mission in life. However, when interacting with some of the key players involved in the change process, I understood that this is only one aspect of it. Mr Chua always put in the forefront the collective character of the whole process. The leadership team of SPS collectively took the responsibility to analyse the situation; identify the need for change; mind-map the direction for change and to finally start "moving the ship." I also realised when using the story and the INSEAD business case in teaching, that groups of international executives from different industries pick up several important lessons that I did not initially think they would consider as important. In this sense, I can also agree with Mr Chua that this story has indeed changed my own perception of leadership and organisations and my way of talking about change management with executives in the classroom.

In the following discussion, I will reflect on a few well known conceptual models that might be helpful in understanding the process. This might add value and help us to appreciate the different aspects of the experience that has changed the lives of many people involved.

When taking over the command of the SPS, Mr Chua analyzed the situation sharply and identified several urgent and pressing issues that needed to be addressed: increasing population of inmates, ageing facilities and the issues of failing to attract and retain enough highly qualified staff. This situation would sooner or later cause real security issues on the ground. Hence, these organisational issues had to be dealt with urgently. Mr Chua and other people of the leadership team insisted that it was these urgent challenges that pushed them into considering the importance of focusing on rehabilitation, rather than the noble reason of doing good to the inmates. However, rather than locking away the inmates in order to protect the society from evil, they decided to focus on developing these human beings into valuable members of society. This new paradigm caused anxiety and psychological insecurity, because of the possibility of the service losing power and identity of the prison officers. This sequence is closely related to the conceptual model of managed organizational change of Edgar Schein (1985, 2004). According to Schein's model, this learning anxiety contains several fears: the fear of temporary incompetence, the fear of punishment for incompetence, the fear of loss of personal identity and the fear of group membership. These four types of fears trigger different forms of defensive responses: Denial, Scapegoating and Bargaining/Maneuvering. Following Schein's recommendations to create psychological safety we can detect many of the measures the leadership team of the SPS has applied in the process (Schein, 2004):

(1) Finding a compelling vision
(2) Organising formal training
(3) Involvement of the learner
(4) Informal training of relevant "family groups" and teams
(5) Practice fields, coaches and feedback
(6) Positive role models

(7) Support groups in which the learning problems can be aired and discussed and
(8) Reward organisational structures consistent with the new paradigm.

In the Captains of Lives story, many of these elements are illustrated. The defensive mechanisms are well documented in the form of the devastating staff survey and other setbacks in the process. The effectiveness of the leadership team in reducing the learning anxiety and creating an environment of psychological safety was most probably due to the various ways in which a large number of the staff were actively involved in the visioning process.Feedback and coaching were officially established and learning sessions (formal and informal) were used in order to support the organisational change. When searching for a positive role model, the leadership team considered various successful organisations. However, the motivational story of *FISH* (Lundin, Paul & Christensen, 2000) about Seattle's Pike Place Fish market really left an impact on the staff. The process of finding a compromise in the visioning process and taking into consideration the security concerns from the governmental officials could be seen as a form of reconciliation between the old and the new organisational culture. According to the conceptual model proposed by Trompennaars and Hampden-Turner (1997), the process of reconciliation is in most cases necessary to achieve a successful transformational change.

However, driving from our research about organisational change at the INSEAD Leadership Center, despite a cognitive analysis of the organisational transformation, many elements are beyond the rational understanding.

Emotions and relationship patterns from the past (individual as much as organizational) can sometimes be helpful in order to understand and demystify the change process (Kets de Vries, 2011). In the Captains of Lives story, one could reflect on the past events that shaped the organisational culture of SPS. Rehabilitation was considered from the early years of SPS to be part of the DNA of the organisation. The other aspect of the change process is systemic: analysing how key players are imbedded in the context of their own personal influencing systems or structures (eg. values or spiritual beliefs) helps understanding how the whole organisation can best connect to its environment. Respecting key relationships to the ministry and using interactions with other organisations like the Police force were instrumental to the success of the transformation process. The so-called *"clinical approach"* to leadership and organisational change (Kets de Vries, 2001) as described above combines the two principal aspects: psychodynamic and systemic.

Understanding the past and present of the system and the people we deal with enables us to shape the future.

Since publishing the INSEAD case study many executives have been exposed to the story. I would like to share some of the reactions managers and leaders have expressed about the Captains of Lives story. The elements participants found most inspiring were the persistence and vision of Mr Chua: challenging the establishment and status quo and managing to make the prison a desirable place to work.

Many executives discovered lessons which could be transferred to their own management of change projects: being surrounded by a motivated and dedicated leadership team, seeking a compromise in order not to lose the momentum of a change process and networking with key members of the staff to achieve a critical mass. Business leaders felt that internal marketing (convincing the staff with doubts) and external marketing (Captains of Lives and Yellow Ribbon Campaign) were the key elements securing the success of the transformation process.

In my opinion, this book about the Captains of Lives is a powerful story because Mr Chua put a real effort to tell the story like it was without adding anything to it and without leaving out major parts. Each reader can identify a facet of the story that applies to his professional reality. Although perhaps targeted at an audience of public service leaders in Asia I would recommend to many Western leaders to look, to learn and to change our mindset regarding change management. Management education can definitely learn many things from an Eastern and Asian approach.

BIBLIOGRAPHY

(1) Schein E (1985). *Organisational Culture and Leadership: A dynamic view*, San Francisco Jossey-Bass.
(2) Schein E (2004). *Organisational Culture and Leadership, Jossey-Bass.*
(3) Lundin S., Paul H. & Christensen J. (2000). *Fish*, Hyperion.
(4) Trompenaats, A & Hampden-Turner (1999). *Riding the Waves of Culture*, New York: McGraw Hill.
(5) Kets de Vries (2011). *The Hedgehog Effect*, John Wiley & Sons.
(6) Kets de Vries (2001). *The Leadership Mystigue*, In London Financial Times, Prentice-Hall.

CONTENTS

NOTES ON ABBREVIATIONS

BEST — Basic Education for Skills Training

CARE — Community Action for the Rehabilitation of Ex-Offenders

CID — Criminal Investigation Department

CDC — Community Development Council

CED — Customs Enforcement Division

CJS — Criminal Justice System

CNB — Central Narcotics Bureau

CPC — Changi Prison Complex

CPC-PMS — Prison Management System at the Changi Prison Complex

CPIB — Corrupt Practices Investigation Bureau

FSC — Family Service Centre

HUMANS — Housing Unit Management System

HWH — Half-way House

ICPA — International Corrections and Prisons Association

ISCOS — Industrial and Services Co-operative Society

ISD — Internal Security Department

JPU — Job Placement Unit

LEA — Law Enforcement Academy

LSI-R — Level of Service Inventory-Revised

MCD — Ministry of Community Development

MCYS — Ministry of Community Development, Youth and Sports

MIT	—	Massachusetts Institute of Technology
NCADA	—	National Council Against Drug Abuse
NCSS	—	National Council for Social Service
NGO	—	Non-government Organisation
NYAA	—	National Youth Achievement Awards
OSY	—	Out-of-school Youth
PAW	—	Play and Wait Programme
PDE	—	Preventive Drug Education
PSC	—	Public Service Commission
R&P	—	Research and Planning
SACA	—	Singapore Aftercare Association
SANA	—	Singapore Anti-Narcotic Association
SCORE	—	Singapore Corporation of Rehabilitative Enterprises
SIR	—	Singapore Immigration & Registration Department (now, ICA, Immigration & Checkpoints Authority)
SPS	—	Singapore Prison Service
SQA	—	Singapore Quality Award
TVC	—	television commercials
WISE	—	Workers Improvement through Secondary Education
VWO	—	Volunteer Welfare Organisation
ZTP	—	Zero Tolerance Policy

INSEAD

Dr Thomas HELLWIG
INSEAD adjunct professor for leadership,
Medical doctor &
executive coach

Dr **Thomas Hellwig** works as an adjunct Professor at INSEAD where he has been associated with the Leadership Centre at INSEAD. He is a trained physician with a doctorate in psychotherapy and an MBA from the INSEAD.

His recent teaching and research focus on change management (team and organisational dynamics), coaching effectiveness and health & stress management. At INSEAD he has also carried out several research projects with Professor Kets de Vries and is a regular presenter at International leadership conferences.

Thomas is of German origin and lives in France. He is regularly involved in assignments throughout Europe, the US and Asia.

CHAPTER ONE

MY ENTRY

When I joined the Civil Service in 1972, I was fresh from a National Service stint and studying in the first year of university in UK on a Public Service Commission (PSC) Scholarship. Little did I realise then that one day, my career in the Civil Service would take me to the Prison Service and I would be instrumental in reforming the prison system.

I joined the Civil Service as an idealistic young man who wanted to serve my country. As a young student, I studied in a Chinese School and was deeply influenced by the Confucian teaching of a gentleman. A Chinese gentleman 君子 is one who despises riches, dismissing money as that awful scent of bronze 铜臭 (in those days, money in China was largely made of bronze). He would gladly die for his emperor and his country (in that order) and he will worry about issues before they reach the people and he will only enjoy the fruits of his own labour after the people have got to enjoy theirs 先天下之忧而忧，后天下之乐而乐. With that kind of ideology, going into the business world was out of the question. It had to wait until I retired from the Civil Service for me to finally try my hand at business. But that is another story.

Fast forward to 1998, I found myself taking over the helm of the Singapore Prison Service after spending the better part of my career in the Singapore Police Force. During my time with the Police from 1977 to 1998, I had gone through most of the critical postings in the Police Force — Head of a regional division, Head of Staff Inspectorate, Director of Systems and Research (this portfolio is now part of the Planning and Organisation Department of the Police), Commander of Traffic Police, Director of Manpower and Administration (now split into Manpower Department and Administration and Finance Department), Director of Training, Director of Operations and Director of Criminal Investigations Department (CID) to name just a few. In between all the Police postings, I had been seconded to the Ministry of Home Affairs as its Director of Operations for 2 years and saw first hand how the political leadership and civil servants interacted and made policies at the highest level.

So in November 1998, fresh from my CID job, I took over from Mr Poh Geok Ek as the Director of Prisons. I was immediately confronted by two pressing issues — overpopulation in prison and shortage of staff due to difficulties in recruitment and retention.

The prison population was then around 16,000 and rising rapidly, putting much strain on the existing infrastructure and resources. It would reach the all time high of more than 18,000 in 2002 before the trend was reversed through reform. Compounding the problem was the fact that very few Singaporeans saw the Prison Service as a viable career choice because of its lacklustre image. The shortage of staff was so severe that the service almost resorted to overseas recruitment to fill the vacancies as a stop-gap measure before this was stopped by political considerations.

CHAPTER ONE

I was aware of these problems while I was still in the Police Force. My predecessor Mr Poh Geok Ek had appealed to the Ministry of Home Affairs to convene a meeting of all the major law enforcement agencies to request that enforcement be slowed down because the prisons could no longer admit prisoners at the prevailing rate. The meeting was arranged but at the meeting, this plea received little sympathy. The consensus at the meeting was that the pace of law enforcement must be dictated by law and order considerations, not by prison capacity. Even if law enforcement agencies slowed down on their enforcement efforts, it would at best be a temporary measure. The expected deterioration of the law and order situation would soon worsen the problem even further. I was at that meeting and I shared this view. This problem of prison over-population needed a more fundamental solution.

Even before I assumed the post, I requested for a number of briefings from the Prison Service to assess the severity of the problems. What I heard was not encouraging. Nobody in the service had any idea how the problems could be tackled. The notion of rehabilitation was raised by my predecessor but the Ministry had rejected his request for a Rehabilitation Division to be formed. The Ministry was not convinced that the huge amount of resources requested for would produce any results. If the Prison Service wanted to experiment with rehabilitation, it would have to do so without extra resources from the government, at least in the beginning until its efficacy was proven.

I learned from the briefings that the over-population in prison was caused primarily by the drug problem and secondarily by the longer sentences imposed by the courts. The law required that drug addicts undergo compulsory "rehabilitation". In practice, this meant that drug addicts were detained administratively until they were deemed to have kicked the habit. It could be anything from 6 months to 2 years. In 1998, just before I came onto the scene, a law was passed to further criminalise repeat drug addicts who had undergone compulsory "rehabilitation" at least twice before. Long prison terms were prescribed for these repeat drug offenders by the Misuse of Drugs Act. They could be imprisoned from 5 to 13 years, depending on the number of times they relapsed. The large number of drug addicts detained in prison was what caused the prison population to explode.

I also found that up to that point in time, the drug rehabilitation programmes were ineffective, with relapse rates far exceeding 50% and reaching as high as 80% for repeat offenders in some years. Prisoners other than those detained for drug abuse had no structured programmes targeted at their rehabilitation. What was understood as rehabilitation by the Prison Service up to that point comprised a tough deterrent regime, work, education, religious services conducted by external volunteers, some vocational skills training and job placement assistance upon release. Faced with the large number of prisoners, these measures failed completely to produce positive change in the prison inmates.

However, there were also some good points and the most important of which was that the discipline among inmates was good despite the very low manning level in prisons. The manning level, measured by the ratio of number of prison staff to the number of inmates was then at around 1 to 8 and rapidly deteriorating. Other plus points were that prison regimes were well structured after many years of evolution and that prison conditions were humane though extremely spartan. One systemic structure I found particularly useful was the oversight system in the form of visiting justices and visitors. These are eminent citizens given access to prisons in order for them to check on the prison conditions and hear prisoners' complaints. This external oversight ensures the integrity of the system. The visiting justices and visitors would later become an important source of feedback to me on how committed the different prisons were to the cause of rehabilitation and how well the programmes were being carried out.

These briefings that I got before assuming the post proper were also useful in showing me what was lacking in the Prison Service. First of all, there was no think-tank of any kind. No officers were assigned full time to do forward looking strategic planning or research to find out what would work for rehabilitation. Secondly, after failing to get additional resources for a rehabilitation division, the Service all but gave up on the idea of rehabilitation. There was only one psychologist in the entire service whose job was to put up standard assessment reports on inmates being considered for discretionary release. The Prison Service then did not possess any intellectual property of note. So before I formally took over the helm, I had already resolved to do two things. One, I would look deeper into the possibility of introducing a formal structure to deliver programmes aimed at creating positive change in the prison inmates. In order to tackle the problem of overcrowding, I must stop the revolving door. Two, I would introduce a forward looking element in the organisation of the service to take up research and planning, and ultimately to develop intellectual properties in the core competency areas of the Prison Service. These two measures, I hoped would help to improve the image of the service from one that just locked people up to one that returned prisoners to society as useful citizens.

CHAPTER TWO

MY INITIAL STEPS

While my preliminary agenda was clear, I had to decide how to deliver on this agenda. I had led a number of change processes in the Police Force prior to my Prison Service posting. My experience had taught me that if I drove my agenda as my own personal agenda, others would seek to undermine it. While I was in CID I had the opportunity of attending a 5-day Learning Organization Course conducted by Daniel Kim and Dianne Corry of Massachusetts Institute of Technology (MIT). They were the disciples of Peter Senge, the author of the book "The Fifth Discipline". The practical guide I learned from them on how to tap the collective wisdom of the organisation would become my method of choice to effect and manage the change. Fresh from leading the change effort in CID, I knew that getting others to buy in on my agenda would also not be sufficient. The best way was to help the leadership team think through our situation together and hope that they would come to the same action agenda as I did. The members of the team would then drive the agenda collectively to achieve wider buy-in. So upon taking over, my first order of business was to assemble that leadership team and create platforms for the team to think through our situation together. I also knew then that taking this approach, I would have to be prepared to let others help shape the agenda.

Upon joining the Prison Service, the first directive that came from my office was to mandate that every officer two levels down within the hierarchy (not counting my deputy) would meet three times a week. Every Monday and Friday, we would meet together for breakfast. However, I was afraid of giving the impression that I took ground commanders away for meetings too frequently. So the superintendents who were in charge of institutions would only have to attend breakfast meetings once a month. The breakfast meeting would be without agenda and its key purpose was for the officers to educate me, an outsider who had never run a prison in his life, about the Prison Service. On Wednesdays, we would meet to consider issues identified at the breakfast meeting formally.

In truth, the breakfast meetings were not solely for my education. It was also a platform for me to assess the quality of the officers that I had. Rumour was then rife that I would be bringing in a team of officers from the Police to run the Prison Service. I must say this did cross my mind. If the officers I had with me in the Prison Service were not up to the task of driving transformational change, then I would certainly have to seek outside help. It was also to be the gift of my time to the senior officers present at the meeting for them to get to understand my principles, my values and my aspirations for the service.

My first impressions of the senior officer corps were favourable. There were a number of bright and idealistic young men and women on the leadership team who were

Chapter Two

very promising. This was so only because in 1991, the then Director of Prisons, Mr Tee Tua Ba put up a very convincing case to the government to bring the terms and conditions of employment in Prison Service up to par with the Police Force. Up till that time, Prison Service pay was on the average 20% below the Police Force. With improved pay and service terms, many good graduates had joined the Prison Service believing that it was a helping profession. Some of them became disappointed and left. However, a large enough number had chosen to remain, hoping to help transform the Prison Service into a true helping profession. Some of them were now in my leadership team. If Mr Tee had not laid this essential ground work, my task would be much more difficult.

However, the number of officers within two levels of me was too large for intimacy. The leadership team would have to be much smaller and we would eventually meet once a month for lunch in addition to the other meetings. It would comprise every officer who had the title of director in their job designation. They were the Deputy Director Lohman Yew, Assistant Director of Operations Jason Wong, and the Assistant Directors of Human Resources and Corporate Services. I would later add to the team the Head of Research and Planning Teo Tze Fang, Head of Intelligence and Head of Programme Lee Kwai Sem, 9 members in all.

Many of the leadership team members who attended my meetings in those early days told me later that it was a traumatic experience for them. In their views, I had applied the interrogation techniques that I learned in criminal investigation on them. I can recall quite vividly a conversation that typified what happened. "I read a book in the last few days on American prisons that referred to inmate clerks. Do we have inmate clerks?" said I. "No, Sir" came the answer. "Why?" "It would not be good for security; we are not sure whether inmates are trustworthy enough?" "Are all of them untrustworthy? Surely some are more trustworthy than others!" I asked again. "We don't have a system to identify the trustworthy ones." "Can we structure one? If the Americans can have it, why can't we?" "We'll look into it, Sir!" "I thought we are short of staff. Wouldn't it be nice if some inmates can be used to share in your workload?" "Yes, it is a good idea, Sir." My final emphatic question would be "when can we finish looking into it?" Some tentative date would be given and I would then put it on record for the matter to be discussed at the formal weekly meeting by that date. The officer responsible for the issue would have to put up a paper for discussion at that meeting.

It was correct to say that I used questioning techniques during my meetings. It was like peeling an onion to get to its core. I needed to know what lay behind all the prison practices or non-practices (what Peter Senge called "mental model", the core assumptions that made up the practice). I needed to bring the officers through the thinking process of assessing our situation in a way that would suggest solutions. It was a time consuming process and that was why we had to meet three times a week. But when the officers came back, it became their ideas that I would approve them for eventual implementation.

Such exchanges were not limited to meetings. In those early days, I made it a point to visit the sixteen prisons all over Singapore to observe first-hand what went on in these prisons and what was right and what was wrong with the way these prisons were managed. My second visit to a prison saw me at the Changi Women's Prison, where one

CHAPTER TWO

of the key early decisions was made to pave the way for the future. I noticed during my visit that the prisoners were asked to face away from me and they were not allowed to look directly at the visitors. I found the officers very brusque when dealing with the inmates. There was much shouting and barking of orders. Upon questioning, I found something that disturbed me profoundly.

I was told that in the past, there were some cases of prison officers being compromised by prisoners to bring in contraband items for them or to perform unwarranted favours. The solution, recommended by the Corrupt Practices Investigation Bureau and adopted by the Prison Service was to minimise contact between officers and inmates to reduce the opportunities available to the inmates to compromise prison officers to do them favours. In fact, officers were rotated amongst different housing units frequently to make sure that they would not become familiar with the prisoners. The result of this was that a mutual distrust developed between officers and inmates. It struck me that this was the mental model that led to the service not having inmate clerks.

Following a sequence of questions and answers similar to the ones on the issue of inmate clerks , I told the officers who accompanied me on the visit that I could not see how we could manage people whom we neither knew well nor cared about. They could not help but agree with me. A decision was taken on the spot to develop a new system of inmate management. The key operating principle was this: every prisoner had to be well known to at least two prison officers. In order to achieve this, each frontline prison officer would be assigned a number of prisoners and become their personal supervisors. These personal supervisors would interact with their charges as often as possible and they had to interview them at least once a month. Personal supervisors would be organised to operate in a fixed team and be supervised by a more senior officer. What remained to be done was to work out the nuts and bolts of the system and that task fell to Jason Wong, the Assistant Director of Operations.

CHAPTER THREE

THE LEAD-UP TO VISIONING

The system that was developed would eventually be known as the Housing Unit Management System or HUMANS for short. The acronym was chosen to signify the shift of emphasis in inmate management to become more inmate-centric. This acronym was only dropped some four years later when the system became the only system of inmate management within the Prison Service and the key plank of inmate management. The decision to stop using the term was also a result of comments from higher quarters that the term suggested that the Prison Service had gone "soft".

In an approach that would typify similar future experiments, the system was not forced on the whole Prison Service immediately. Rather, it was discussed at the various meetings and only the superintendents of institutions who believed in its merit were asked to volunteer their prisons to test out the system. Four prisons came on board in the first wave, and all of them chose to experiment with the system in one or two housing units before implementing it throughout the whole prison. The staff soon realised that in addition to making rehabilitation a possibility, HUMANS was actually beneficial to intelligence gathering, security, discipline, control and management. The closer contact with inmates often gave early alerts to potential problems between different inmates and different groups of inmates so that problems could be nipped in the bud. The early adopters soon spread the word around but progress was slow. It would take three years for the whole Prison Service to embrace the system. Because of the extra demands placed on staff by HUMANS, the use of inmates to assist prison officers as stewards (we decided against the use of the term inmate clerks) became a necessity. Outsourcing of certain functions like escorting prisoners out to court and to hospital also helped to free up manpower for the experiment. Does this initiative increase the likelihood that prison officers might be compromised? Of course it does. This problem was addressed by the setting up of the Ethics structure, which will be dealt with later in Chapter 9.

It soon became clear to me that HUMANS was no panacea. In fact, without the existing mental models being fundamentally challenged and uprooted, rehabilitation would be a forlorn hope. I decided that the way to do this was to conduct a visioning exercise. Following the well documented methodology of Peter Senge, we needed to go through the process of answering three key questions in order to produce a strategic plan and create a different future for the Prison Service. These questions were: Where are we now? Where do we want to go? How do we get there?

The answers to the first two questions would reveal the gaps between the current reality and the vision and that would engender the creative tension for the last question to be tackled. The vision deployment matrix was another tool that could be used. Each of the situations in the current reality had to be understood in terms of the vision at work, the mental model at work, the systemic structure, the patterns and the events that showed up the situation. Similarly, in answering the last two questions, the vision element, the desired mental model, the systemic structure, the patterns and the events that we expected to see had to be visualised.

I turned to Teo Tze Fang, Jason Wong's assistant in the Operations Division to head the newly created Research and Planning branch (hereafter referred to as R&P). I asked Tze Fang to pick the best and brightest young officers for the branch to help him in his first task of driving the visioning exercise to answer the three strategic questions. The first objective of visioning was to produce an end-state vision statement that would embody how the Prison Service would like to see itself in the distant future. Since everyone needed some clarity on how distant a future we were talking about, I decided to use twenty years. The process must involve every prison officer who had a view on that future. I told the leadership team quite clearly that since I would not be in that future — I would be due for retirement in nine years' time — the vision could not be mine. The people who are expected to be in that future must be the ones to decide. I would merely play the role of facilitator and consultant to steer the exercise.

Quite by coincidence, we had set upon a date in May 1999 to have the Prison Service's Work Plan Seminar. The Work Plan Seminar was an annual major event in the planning cycle of all major agencies under the Ministry of Home Affairs. As it happened, the Prison Service had not had one for a few years and I decided that we must revive it. However, unlike previous seminars, I wanted this particular seminar to be a key platform on which the first ideas about the desired vision were articulated. In order to ensure that the outcome of the Work Plan Seminar would be fruitful, I asked R&P to form three working groups each to be led by a Superintendent of Prison or a senior staff officer in the lead-up to the seminar. Each of the working groups would ponder over the answers to one question and present their thinking at the Seminar. The questions they were asked to think about were: Where are we now? What is wrong with us? Where do we want to go? Two of the questions are the same as the ones I mentioned two paragraphs ago but with one additional question. The reason for this was that the "how to get there" question could only be answered after the vision question had been answered and that would be addressed only after the vision had become clear. I wanted the "what is wrong" question to give some inkling on the possible starting points for the change journey.

The three working groups were working on a very tight deadline of three months. It was obvious from the beginning that the first two groups were going along at a brisk pace. However, the last group was stuck and could not move from square one for a few weeks. Whatever they produced in those few weeks was confusing, amorphous and lacked conviction. Tze Fang came bearing the bad news to me and I decided to have a brainstorming session with the group in order to fulfil my facilitator cum consultant role. I told the group to use imagery to express their ideals for the service. After all, we were after an end-state picture. They should therefore think pictorially and metaphorically rather than in words alone. The session put renewed energy into the group, which was led by a social work trained officer Abdul Karim. A few weeks later, they presented their answer to the question to me. It was indeed a picture — a drop of water entering a larger body of water and creating a ripple. Each ring of the ripple represented a people group. At the core was the staff, the next ring was the inmates, after that, inmates' family, the criminal justice system, then the community, and the outermost ring was nation and beyond and it rippled to eternity. (Please see Figure 1 below.)

This picture of a ripple was a wonderful and powerful summation of the group's aspiration. It encapsulated ambitions that even I, up to that point, did not quite dare to dream of. It said that in order to create positive change in inmates, it must all start with the prison staff. They must be willing to commit to the task of reforming inmates. But that would not be enough. The ripple must next touch the

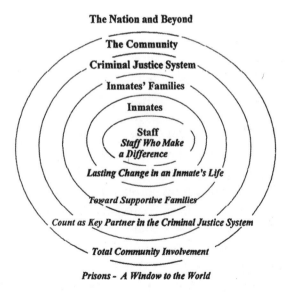

Figure 1: The ripple effect of the six stakeholders and the proposed vision mark.

inmates to motivate them to change. Then the inmates' families would come into the picture to give the inmates the love and support that they need to complete their change journey. Then the criminal justice system must take cognisance of the need to rehabilitate offenders in enforcement policies and sentencing. The ripple must then touch the community to accept released inmates back to society and give them equal opportunities and second chances to become contributing citizens. The ripple could then touch the whole nation and even other nations to cause them to recognise the positive role that rehabilitation could play. To be honest, the result was far beyond what I could think of or hope for. This picture of the ripple would eventually manifest itself in various aspects of our strategic articulation. The power of collective wisdom burst onto the scene for the first time in the prison reform journey, but many more such miraculous moments were to follow.

The presentations of the three groups caused a tremendous buzz at the Work Plan Seminar. I was also pleasantly surprised that my Minister decided to stay back to listen to the presentations instead of leaving us after his opening speech as was customary. Riding on the momentum, I invited all prison officers to voice their views on the presentations in focus groups and online chat rooms after the seminar. All in all, more than 700 out of the 2000 staff gave their views and ideas. R&P collated all the inputs and proceeded to invite around 250 staff with the most interesting views to join us in a two-day retreat to craft the vision statement. Many of the officers invited were junior frontline officers. To ensure that rank would be no barrier to speaking one's mind, officers would attend the retreat in civilian clothes. In a hierarchical organisation like the Prison Service, junior officers were

CHAPTER THREE

usually expected to execute ideas of the senior officers and not to articulate their own. Their participation in the Work Plan Seminar, the focus groups and online chats and now the vision retreat heralded a complete break with the past. This would culminate in the merger of the senior and junior officers' clubs a few years later. From then on, junior officers no longer just did as they were told. They were accepted as thinking individuals whose views should get equal airing. Whether an idea would be adopted depended on the quality of the idea, not the rank of the person who espoused it.

CHAPTER FOUR

VISIONING

There was a tremendous amount of goodwill, commitment and enthusiasm at the visioning retreat. I cannot quite remember how the maritime flavour seeped into the vision. I believed it had something to do with the starfish story contained in a training video first shown at the Work Plan Seminar. This was the synopsis of the video: "An old man was walking on a beach dotted with countless starfish one morning. He noticed a boy picking up starfish one by one and gently throwing them back into the sea. When asked why, the boy explained that the stranded starfish would die if left to lie in the morning sun. 'But there are millions of starfish on this beach,' said the old man. 'How can you make a difference?' The boy picked up another starfish and threw it back to the sea. 'It makes a difference to this one.' The starfish story would exert a lasting influence in the Prison Service and re-told many times after the Work Plan Seminar. When I left the Prison Service in 2007, among the parting gifts I received was a starfish made of clay in a wooden frame from an inmate. It was accompanied by a tribute which still moves me today.

The pace of the retreat was frenetic. Those present were divided into groups to work on the six vision markers in the ripple picture presented at the Work Plan Seminar. These markers were: staff who make a difference, lasting change in an inmate's life, towards supportive families, count as a key partner in criminal justice system, total community mobilisation, prison service as the compass for corrections. Groups worked overnight to harvest the best and boldest ideas, clustered them and crafted statements around them. On the morning of the second day, the various groups presented their final products to the leadership team.

It was an exciting and painful session all at once. The endless arguments for and against the inclusion of certain ideas during the first two days re-surfaced. It was obvious that there was too much divergence and not enough efforts to forge convergence. It then fell on me to arbitrate and integrate what I thought were the best ideas. Finally, after a long morning, the group managed to craft a vision statement. It read: "We aspire to be captains in the lives of offenders committed to our care. We will be instrumental in steering profound change in them together with their families and the community. We will thus be the compass for corrections." The meeting also decided to adopt the vision tagline: "Captains of Lives" and the vision logo of a steering wheel. The mission statement was also revised. It then read: "As a key partner in Criminal Justice, we protect society through the safe custody and rehabilitation of offenders, co-operating in prevention and aftercare."

The choice of the maritime metaphor for the vision statement was not a unanimous one. In the end, I had to exercise my casting vote in favour of it. I am a landlubber who has no great fondness for the sea. However, I was inspired by the starfish story and I thought the metaphor of a captain steering a ship was a very good picture of a prison officer trying to help a prisoner change. You can only point the ship in the right direction but you cannot ensure that it gets to its destination. The rest depends on the elements, the seaworthiness of the ship and the skills of the crew.

The vision statement thus crafted should settle once and for all the end-state that we were working towards but that relief proved to be premature. I wanted the statement to be publicly unveiled to commit the service and the government to the cause. The families of inmates and the community at large also needed to be enrolled into the vision for it to work. Since we had the aspiration to spread the ideal to the nation and beyond, having it as an internal statement would not do. I therefore needed not only to persuade my parent ministry to approve the mission and vision statements but also the minister to unveil it. I even settled on a date for the unveiling, the eve of the new millennium, 31 December 1999. The unveiling would coincide with the ground-breaking ceremony of the Changi Prison Complex to add poignancy to the occasion.

The idea of centralising all the prisons at one prison complex in Changi was broached out of sheer necessity during the tenure of my predecessor Mr Poh Geok Ek. It was obvious to him that the population explosion of prisoners required new prison capacity to be built. However, previous attempts at securing land for new prisons had met with problems. Whenever there was competing use for land, the land earmarked for new prisons would have to give way to other uses. An official in the Ministry of Home Affairs then broached the idea of re-developing the biggest piece of land the current prisons sat on in Changi.

Since some of the prisons were already there, there would be no competing demand for the land. The extra capacity would be created by building upward and by acquiring adjoining land parcels that were as yet undeveloped. My predecessor had already settled on the blue print of the complex. 15 prisons would be built, each independent of the others with its own perimeter security buffer land and security fencing.

When I first saw this blueprint, I thought something was amiss. The security buffers required for each of the 15 prisons meant that the available land was not used optimally. Also, more could be done to reap economies of scale. Why should 15 prisons located together each have its own kitchen, security system and sick bay? Surely, these facilities could be centralised and scaled up. I wanted a real complex instead, with integrated operations, logistical systems and security systems. However, I recognised the merit of separating the complex into a number of clusters. After one cluster was built and operated for a period of time, we could then learn from the mistakes made in the earlier cluster before building the next cluster. I knew it was impossible not to make mistakes when you are doing something new. The important thing is to learn from the mistakes and not repeat them on a more massive scale.

This decision to develop the Changi Prison Complex in clusters proved to be prescient. We did make some mistakes in the first cluster. For example, the area provided for the gate was too small. As a result, only one vehicle could get through at a time. We did not correctly predict the traffic volume that would go through the gate and serious traffic jam was the result. This lesson was well learned in the building of the second cluster.

CHAPTER FOUR

The other pressing reason to revise the blueprint was the change that was then taking place to embrace rehabilitation. The new infrastructure must support the new strategy. Once the infrastructure was cast in concrete, we would not be able to make any changes without great cost and effort.

The planning team for the re-development did not understand me initially. They were livid about having to go back to the drawing board. The first revision produced a blueprint that grouped all the maximum security prisons in one cluster, medium security in two other clusters and minimum security in the fourth cluster. It was rejected by me for two reasons. Firstly, if all the clusters comprised prisons of the same security classification, all of them would be alike and prisoners would not be able to be transferred to a lower security setting within the same cluster, complicating the operating procedure. More importantly, each cluster would be different from the previous one and there would be no opportunity to learn the lessons from the first cluster in the building of the next cluster. After much angst and derision, the team finally delivered a blueprint that called for four clusters of five prisons each with different security levels within the same cluster. I accepted the proposal just in time for the Work Plan Seminar in May. The race to complete the detailed infrastructural planning and then synchronise the ground-breaking ceremony for the complex with the unveiling of the vision statement was now on.

CHAPTER FIVE

RE-VISIONING

The rejection of our proposed vision statement by the Ministry of Home Affairs came in the form of an email. To most officers in the agencies and departments, the Ministry was a somewhat amorphous entity. However, as I had worked in the Ministry for two years from October 1990 to September 1992, I could usually make a good guess as to who was behind a certain decision from the Ministry. In this case, the rejection did not surprise me but its tone did. Just to introduce the cast at the Ministry, at the top was the Minister for Home Affairs, Mr Wong Kan Seng. This is the man who introduced the legislation criminalising repeated drug offenders. Reputed to be tough as nails, he was known for coming down hard on crime and being tenacious in the pursuit of policies to safeguard the security of Singapore. He was assisted by Professor Ho Peng Kee, the Minister of State (*de facto* deputy minister). Professor Ho is a true humanitarian, a good foil to the Minister. The politicians were supported by civil servants who were both the politicians' think-tank and executives. The Head of the civil servants in the Ministry was Mr Peter Chan, the Permanent Secretary. He was a man with great intellect and given to introspection.

All correspondence from the Ministry was issued on behalf of the Permanent Secretary but most key decisions were made or at least concurred with by the Minister.

The main reason for the rejection was that the vision statement completely omitted any mention of secure custody. Its singular focus on rehabilitation was unacceptable to the Ministry. A number of amendments were suggested to relegate rehabilitation to be second in importance behind security and I was to revert to the Ministry how I proposed to amend the vision statement. In subsequent meetings and conversations, Ministry officials intimated that the bosses felt that the vision statement gave the impression that the Prison Service had gone soft.

The version proposed by the Ministry read: "We will ensure the safe custody of offenders, and together with their family and the community, facilitate their return to society as law-abiding citizens. We will be an exemplary prison service." What was glaring in the Ministry's version was that it omitted any mention of "captains of lives", the most important phrase in the entire statement.

Upon receiving the bad news, I had an opportunity to inform the leadership team during our regular breakfast meeting the next morning. I told the meeting about the Ministry's firm rejection of our proposed vision statement and the suggested amendments. It was clear from the tone of the Ministry's reply that they were not enthusiastic about the idea of rehabilitation and wanted to water it down as much as possible. This meant that if we proceeded to try out rehabilitation and failed, [our heads would be on the chopping block].

CHAPTER FIVE

I looked around the room and observed the body language of the assemblage. I saw many frightened faces, hunched shoulders but some defiant looks as well. I said: "You know the vision statement was not mine. It was the collective ideal of many of us. As your leader, I am prepared to put my head on the chopping block to defend our ideal. But you must be prepared to offer your head with mine. How many of you would?" There was a pregnant silence for a few seconds and then a voice rang out: "My head is with yours, Sir." That punctuated the silence and one by one, all present contributed their heads. I knew at that point that there was no turning back. We went on to discuss how we should respond to the Ministry and I immediately started to craft my reply after the meeting.

The first draft of my reply was combative and some-what impolite. When I finished the draft, I thought I should not send it immediately but give myself time to calm down before attempting another draft. So I slept on the matter (I did not get much sleep that night) and the next morning, I re-visited the draft to make it as tactful as possible, yet displaying the resolve to experiment with rehabilitation. I then asked Tze Fang and Jason to look through the draft and they suggested some more amendments to tone down the angst. Eventually, I sent out the carefully crafted reply to the Ministry.

In it, I explained that it was never our intention to abandon our focus on security. This was in fact taken care of in the mission statement. The vision statement was intended by us to paint an end-state picture of the Prison Service and it would become our collective ideal to achieve that end-state. We wanted to embrace rehabilitation and experiment with it. We were not absolutely confident that we would succeed but there was no other alternative that we could think of to deal with our present situation. I went on to say that because the vision statement was the collective effort of many officers over many months, I could not just amend it on my own, and neither should the Ministry. I proposed to have another visioning session with the officers involved in the earlier session that produced the vision statement but this time, with representatives from the Ministry present so that the Ministry could feel the pulse of the Prison Service. That would also give us an opportunity to amend the statement so that it would be mutually acceptable. I also proposed that the session should have an independent facilitator to ensure that there would not be a shouting match between the adversarial parties and that there would be a genuine dialogue to break the impasse.

The re-visioning took place in November 1999 with Aubeck Kam from the Police Force as facilitator. Ministry representatives were present together with some 200 of the officers involved in the first visioning retreat. That the session came to a successful conclusion was in no small part due to the skills of the facilitator. The opportunity for a direct dialogue between Prison Officers and Ministry officials produced a positive result and a viable compromise. The mission statement was untouched while the vision statement was amended to read: *"We aspire to be captains in the lives of offenders committed to our custody. We will be instrumental in steering them towards being responsible citizens with the help of their families and the community. We will thus build a secure and exemplary prison system."*

Given the circumstances, that was the best compromise we could have. The Ministry would allow us to experiment with rehabilitation but we had to commit ourselves to bringing security to a world class level. With that compromise, we were now able to move full steam ahead with the strategy and initiatives to bring us closer to the vision. The compromise was struck in time for the public unveiling of the vision and mission statements and the ground-breaking ceremony of the Changi Prison Complex on the eve of the millennium, 31 December 1999. It was a new dawn indeed for the Prison Service as well as thousands of prisoners both current and future.

CHAPTER SIX

THE PRISON SCHOOL

At the threshold of the millennium, another dawn of sorts was breaking in the Prison Service. The new Prison School was to open its doors to inmate students on 3 January 2000.

Even before the visioning exercise was completed, my staff and I were busy thinking up new ideas to further the cause of rehabilitation. We could not allow things to grind to a halt while waiting for the visioning exercise to be completed. We needed to free up resources as much as possible for new initiatives that would soon emanate from the visioning process and the HUMANS system being experimented with right then. So we started to look for new areas where efficiency could be maximised and where we could score a quick win on rehabilitation. This would prepare the ground for the all-out push toward the vision.

Education was one such possible area. In 1999, the Prison Service already had a pool of 22 teachers — 12 trained teachers seconded from the Ministry of Education and 10 so-called part-time teachers who were actually full-time employees recruited to teach inmate students but who were not certified by the Ministry of Education.

Every prison would have some make-shift classrooms and these teachers would go around to all the prisons to discharge their teaching duties. Because of the small number of students in each prison, a teacher would only have a handful of students in his class. A lot of the teachers' time was spent on getting from one prison to another. Teachers were not properly supervised and had little opportunity to interact among themselves and with the Prison Officers in charge of the inmate students. As a result, very few inmates had the opportunity to study in prison. Even when they did, the learning was not at the same level as a mainstream school.

Another major downside of such an arrangement was that students were a small minority among the inmates. Many people in prison were those who despised academic pursuits. Because of this, the general population of inmates did not take to the students kindly. Even the Prison Officers in charge of these student inmates shared the same negative attitude and did not give them much help to facilitate their learning, neither were they empowered to do so. In a normal prison environment, it was well nigh impossible for inmate students to hit the books with any single-mindedness. A prison school, centralising all the teachers and students in one location would solve both problems. It would increase the number of student places greatly and create an environment fit for academic pursuits. Education could then become a key part of the rehabilitation effort. There was enough evidence from researches done in other countries to show that education gave released prisoners the prerequisites for skills upgrading, which in turn helped them to secure their livelihood and break out of a criminal lifestyle. The logic was compelling, or so we thought.

CHAPTER SIX

However, the proposal met with strong headwind when it went through the approval process in the Ministry. The Ministry feared that an idea like this would cost too much to implement. This was in spite of the fact that we proposed to convert a small prison, which was itself converted from a disused primary school into the Prison School. We promised to spend as little as possible on renovation and conversion. It was obvious to me that the Ministry was objecting not because the logic of the proposal was flawed, but because of something more fundamental. The Prison School idea would mean that the Prison Service would commit itself to running education in prison seriously and professionally, which was not the case hitherto. Being the Ministry in charge of security matters, and not education, the Ministry probably did not see this as something that should be on their plate.

However, the compelling logic won the day in the end. Again, we were (almost grudgingly) allowed to experiment with the idea. After spending about $600,000 to convert the Kaki Bukit Prison into the Kaki Bukit Centre (Prison School), the school opened its doors to 160 students for the 2000 academic year. The students would pursue N, O and A level studies and take part in the national examinations at the end of the year. For readers outside Singapore, I need to explain that secondary education in Singapore normally ends with the O level certificate after four years of schooling. However, for weaker students who do not do well in their first two years of secondary school, they will sit for the N level at the end of the two years and if they do well enough, they will then be able to study an extra year leading to the O level, a total of five years of schooling for such students. Another two years of studies would lead to the A level, a level required for entry into university.

The Prison School did not have the luxury of giving students six or seven years of schools. Students were selected for each level based on their academic achievements before admission to prison and an entrance test to determine their suitability to be placed at a certain level. Students had to pay the examination fees but those who could not do so could apply for the fees to be paid from donations and later from the Yellow Ribbon Fund. One might ask what about the offenders below or above these levels. Inmates could still enrol in BEST (Basic Education for Skills Training) and WISE (Workers Improvement through Secondary Education) courses at most institutions and these were targeted at those below N level. These courses were national courses developed for workforce improvement and they were conducted in prison by external service providers to bring lowly educated inmates up to speed to be deployed for work. Prison Service does not fund tertiary level courses and students taking tertiary level courses would normally do so through correspondence and pay their own fees. The Prison School also offered technical education for students to pursue the National Technical Certificates. A classroom for technical education was structured for that specific purpose.

From the start, we decided that the school would operate on the principle of "school first, prison second". It would not just focus on academic studies; it would also run co-curricular activities, most of which would be rehabilitative in nature. The school piloted many innovative rehabilitative programmes. These included: the National Youth Achievement Awards (NYAA) programme, Core Skills Programme, Specialised Treatment Programme, Family Involvement Programme and Peer Support Programme. It offered among others, music, drama, broadcasting, dance, acrobatic, sports, arts and IT training as co-curricular activities. It piloted the first radio and TV station for internal broadcast of prison news and education programmes to prisoners.

I would touch on the Core Skills Programme and Specialised Treatment Programme in the next chapter. The Family Support Programme enrolled the family members of the students in their road to rehabilitation. Families would be kept informed of the progress of the students. At key junctures of the students' development, families were invited to visit and talk to their loved ones and witness their achievements. The Peer Support Programme identified the stronger students to act as peer tutors to the weaker students. These tuitions typically took place in the evening outside of curriculum time. Apart from helping students achieve better academic results and develop their characters, these programmes and co-curricular activities also ensured that a student's day was fully occupied even on Saturdays and Sundays when there were no classes.

One of the new practices in the prison school was for teachers and staff to identify and address an inmate by name, and not by his prison number. It might seem like a small matter but in truth, it was an important milestone to embrace rehabilitation. It had long been a practice for a prison inmate to be addressed by staff by his prison number. In fact, the shirts worn by inmates had only their prison numbers emblazoned on the chest. This was done to strip prisoners of their individualities so that they become just one of the prisoners, regardless of who they were in normal lives. This new practice gave inmates back their individual identities, recognising them as individuals with different needs, different personalities requiring different treatments to achieve rehabilitation. The practice would later be adopted throughout the service.

On the school side of the house, the Prison School adopted a disciplinary process for the students called Responsible Thinking Process. A few other mainstream schools also piloted this process at around the same time. For the Prison School, this move was especially significant because otherwise, the students who committed minor infractions in class would have to be subjected to the more severe prison disciplinary process. When a student needed to be disciplined for minor infractions, they were asked to reflect on what they had done wrong. They did so by sitting in a small square drawn in the middle of an empty room. They were asked to think about what they had done wrong, why they did it, the consequence of what they did (for example, disrupting the class and affecting the studies of their classmates) and formulate a plan to prevent any recurrence. The plan would have to state what targets they would set for themselves and they would be monitored to see if they achieved the targets. The completed plan would then be submitted for approval and follow up.

Over the years, the school went from strength to strength, becoming a living laboratory to experiment with new and innovative rehabilitative programmes before they were introduced service wide. The academic results of the students in the Prison School were on par with mainstream schools and even above par in some years. I think the key advantage of studying in prison is that there are no distractions. There is no night life, no entertainment outlets or eateries to while time away, and most importantly, no members of the opposite sex. The environment was designed with one single purpose, to create an environment conducive to studying. Such an environment also makes it possible to introduce more varied co-curricular activities, such as broadcasting and acrobatic.

CHAPTER SIX

In fact, the variety of co-curricular activities is only limited by the volunteers who had the know-how available to run them. Volunteers are such a key part to the success of the whole rehabilitation endeavour that we would later form a unit in the Programme Branch to take charge of volunteer affairs. Both my daughters would later volunteer themselves to teach in the Changi Women's Prison branch of the Prison School in support of their old man's cause. Many of their prison students continued to be in contact with them even after they were released. I learned a great deal from them about the difficulty a released inmate faced and the reality of aftercare.

The student intake increased markedly after a few years from the initial 160 to more than 300 in some years. Students' profiles also changed from mainly young offenders to include a significant number of adults. Many of the students would never have been able to study in a proper school if they had not ended up in prison. Adult education became one of the emphases of the school. Apart from assessing the students academically to see if they were suitable for the school, there were three other restrictions on who would qualify for the school. They must be male, classified Class B on the rehabilitation assessment tool (this would be explained in greater detail in the next chapter) and medium to low risk on the security assessment tool. Because of these restrictions, the school had to have branches in the women's prison (only one in Singapore and where my daughters volunteered their services) and a maximum security prison.

However, the sterling results achieved by Prison School students in national examinations failed to impress the Ministry and from time to time, I would get queries on why we were spending so much on the school. This happened every time we asked for funds to improve the facilities. Somehow, we managed to get what we needed and the school had a science laboratory (we did not offer chemistry because of the obvious security risk), and a new block which contained all the facilities for the co-curricular activities I mentioned before. One highlight of every academic year was the presentation of the NYAA awards. The NYAA Council became a key partner of the Prison School and they would always try to invite a cabinet minister to be the guest-of-honour to give away the awards. Of course, we would always conduct a visit of the school for the guest-of-honour. This proved to be very important as more ministers became impressed with what we were doing and gave us behind-the-scene support for our initiatives. Some of them became active advocates for us through the Yellow Ribbon Project.

In one particular instance, the then Minister For Education was the guest-of-honour. He was thoroughly impressed with the school and what it was doing. He was particularly impressed with the students who briefed him during the visit. After the visit, he wrote an email to my Minister expressing his surprise at how well the school was doing and how well the students acquitted themselves when briefing him during his visit. His glowing assessment, however, did not bring about the expected response from my Minister. My Minister actually asked me to review the rationale of having the school and examine whether we had spent too much to maintain the school. His displeasure came as a surprise and to this day, I have no explanation for it. I had to reiterate the rationale for having the school and the fact that the economy of scale reaped from centralising the teaching resources actually led to savings rather than wastage. The Minister reluctantly let the matter rest. That was in

2006, seven years after his encouraging presence at the 1999 Work Plan Seminar had emboldened me to launch out into uncharted waters for the Prison Service.

By 2006, the momentum of the new rehabilitative approach had become unstoppable as many key partners in various sectors rallied around the cause. By then, the Prison School had attracted hundreds of volunteers to contribute their time and talent to help students in numerous spheres of endeavours.

CHAPTER SEVEN

THE REHABILITATION FRAMEWORK

By the time the Prison School opened its doors, the rehabilitation framework had been largely developed. Being the central plank of my original agenda, I could not wait for the visioning process to be completed before developing ideas about how to carry out rehabilitation. In fact, some work had been done by my predecessor Mr Poh Geok Ek. Although there was no R&P (Research and Planning branch) then, Mr Poh had assigned a few staff officers to conduct a thorough search of the literature on the topic of rehabilitation of offenders prior to proposing the setting up of a rehabilitation division to the Ministry. Thus, the organisation had been up to speed on the theoretical aspects of such a venture. However, since there was a lack of practical experience, the Ministry had refused to channel resources into something which they regarded as uncertain and unproven in the Asian context. I knew that I had to start experimenting on our own steam without asking for additional resources, at least initially. Frankly, at that point in time, I was unconvinced myself and I needed to have a first-hand look at a correctional system that had successfully carried out rehabilitation. So in May 1999, I led a team to the United Kingdom and Canada to study their respective rehabilitation systems.

The main destination of the trip was Canada, which was reputed to be the most advanced correctional system in the world. We also went to the UK because the system in Singapore was very much a British legacy and I wanted to see what the British had done in the modern era to their prison system. The Canadians managed to convince me that their cognitive behavioural approach towards rehabilitation (which was premised upon what goes on in the mind affects behaviour) did indeed work and we took away a lot of knowledge and lessons from Canada. There were, however, a few things that disturbed me. When I visited a prison in Montreal, I found that the custodial officers were on strike. The reason was they did not want to take on additional duties that required them to play a part in the rehabilitation process. I learned that rehabilitation or treatment, as the Canadians called it, was the duty of the probation officers. However, without co-operation from the custodial staff, the probation officers' efforts were undermined.

I learned from the officers with me that some years ago, the Singapore Prison Service also experimented with rehabilitation of young offenders. A separate group of officers, called living-quarters officers were assigned to this job. The service encountered exactly the same problem experienced by the Canadians. The two groups of officers just could not see eye-to-eye for reasons of turf and professional pride. I resolved then that in our experiment with rehabilitation, we would not use a separate group of officers. The prison officers would have to play the dual role of controller and counsellor. I did not agree with the Canadian officials I talked to that the two roles could not mix. If one has been a parent, one would have experienced the need to play this dual role to one's children. I believed that the ability to both discipline and nurture must be innate. All that needed to be done was to draw on this innate ability and develop it into a professional skill. The subsequent development of the rehabilitation system in Singapore proved me right.

The other thing that disturbed me was, Canada had some 200 psychologists supporting their treatment effort and they had a staff to inmate ratio better than 1 to 1. In the Singapore Prison Service, we had only 1 psychologist and a staff to inmate ratio of 1 to 8. We must therefore think of some ways to do what the Canadians did without a sevenfold increase in headcount. Such an increase in headcount would not be supported by the Ministry. Even if it was supported, we would not be able to find the number of new employees in Singapore's tight labour market. It was however clear to me that we could not continue to have only one psychologist in the service and we needed to set up a proper Psychological Service Branch.

Teo Tze Fang and Shie Yong Lee were two of the officers who accompanied me on the trip and it was down to them and their team in R&P to propose a way forward. We had discussed the conceptual framework during and after our trip. I wanted them to look at using the assessment tool Level of Service Inventory-Revised (hereafter referred to as LSI-R), which the Canadians used to determine the intensity of treatment required by an offender as a classification tool. Class A would be those whose risk level of re-offending was low enough not to require treatment. Class C would be those whose risk level was too high for the modest resources we had. We would only focus our efforts on those in between, assessed to be Class B where we would have the best return on our investment.

Tze Fang and his team went about their work with a single-mindedness that greatly impressed me. They decided that the first task was to make sure the LSI-R worked in Singapore as well as in Canada. So they picked a sample of prisoners whose risk level we knew (because they had re-offended) or whose risk level we could guess at well enough (because of their behaviour in prison), and applied the LSI-R on them to see if the results were as expected. They were. The next task was to adjust the actuarial table or curve to the local population. LSI-R consists of a set of questions designed to uncover the various risk factors in a prisoner's life that would be predictive of his re-offending. The score is reflective of the level of risk. The actual risk level is determined by fitting the score onto an actuarial curve drawn using historical data. So for a score of say, 20, one could read off the curve to determine that the risk of re-offending within two years of release from prison was 33%. In different societies, the actuarial curve would be slightly different. R&P then conducted a norming study on an enlarged sample of prisoners to determine the shape of the actuarial curve among Singaporean offenders. This work was completed by the time the Prison School was ready so that prospective students could be assessed before admission.

In practice, this was how the framework operated on the ground. When a person first entered prison, he would be assessed for his security risk and his rehabilitation potential. Security risk was determined by looking at his antecedence and prison record. A security assessment tool was later developed to do the assessment more rigorously. If he was deemed a person inclined to the use of violence or a potential flight risk, he would be assigned a higher security level. There were a total of four security levels, 1 being the highest and 4 the lowest. Rehabilitation potential was determined by the use of LSI-R. Initially, only prisoners serving a sentence of one year and above were subject to assessment. They were classified into Classes A, B and C. Prisoners not classified because of their short sentences and those on remand were assigned Class D. The inmates were then placed in a particular institution according to their classification. For example, a prisoner who had the classification of 1A would end up in a maximum security prison.

Part of the classification process also determined the personal route map of an inmate. The route map would plan his passage through prison, the skills training programmes and rehabilitation programmes that he should take part in to meet his rehabilitation needs and where and when he would be deployed for work. The first programme to be developed to address rehabilitation needs was the Core Skills Programme. All inmates including Class D inmates were eligible to take part in this programme which addressed basic needs like anger management and stress management. Next, Specialised Treatment Programmes were developed to address different needs, addictions and according to different offender profiles. These programmes were rolled out progressively on an experimental basis before being implemented throughout the whole prison system.

These first tentative steps in trying out rehabilitation later matured into a sophisticated system of assessment, treatment and rehabilitation. I shall have a little more to say about this in Chapter 13.

CHAPTER EIGHT

STRATEGY TO ACHIEVE VISION

Once the vision and mission statements were finalised, we wasted no time to brainstorm on how to plug the gaps between the vision and the current reality. This was done again in early 2000 by way of a task force of the key staff members whose views had proven to be useful in the visioning exercise. The work of the task force would pave the way for the 2000 Work Plan Seminar. At this point, we started to run into some methodological difficulties. The literature on learning organisation typified (but not limited to) by Peter Senge's book "The Fifth Discipline", which we had been using to guide us in our visioning hitherto, was not specific enough to shed light on how we should proceed from where we were. The problem of steering the organisation in a new direction was enormous and the literature did not give us sufficient guidance on how to break down the problem. One day, while doing some mental callisthenic to try and find a solution, it dawned upon me that we could map the six vision markers against the functional areas identified in the mission statement. Each box of the two-dimensional matrix would be a component of the larger problem but it would become more manageable to grasp intellectually. I suggested this newly invented method to the task force. The task force was then broken down into groups to consider each box of the matrix in turn. A sub-set of the results is given in Annex A as an illustration.

The task force achieved many breakthroughs in thinking. The "throughcare" concept (caring for offenders from admission into prison till up to six months after release) was mooted for the first time as well as the need for family work. The role of SCORE (Singapore Corporation of Rehabilitative Enterprises) loomed large and we realised for the first time that we needed to get this strategic partner on board before we could achieve real throughcare. We also began to understand how important it was to engage the judiciary and enforcement agencies so that they could understand our work and aspirations. Many of the ideas generated then were so paradigm changing that they were not fully implemented even till this day.

To readers outside of Singapore, I should explain what SCORE is. It is a company established by an act of Parliament to take charge of the prison industry as well as skills training for prison inmates. Such a company is known as a statutory board. The company has its own management which is separate from the Prison Service. The only linkage until then was that the Director of Prisons also served as a director in the SCORE board. The rationale for this arrangement was to give the company some freedom and agility outside the civil service rules so that it could function as a business entity without being hampered by the bureaucracy. I think SCORE is one of the very few companies running prison industries in the world that is completely self-sufficient and does not require regular injections of public funds.

Over the years, SCORE also took on some aftercare functions. For example, to ensure that prison inmates made use of the vocational skills they acquired in prison, SCORE took on a job placement function. This arrangement of having a different agency to manage the prison industry made a lot of business sense. However, the downside was, the prison management and SCORE management might not always share the same vision and aspiration. That was a problem and I realised that I had to deal with it soon enough.

The task force's work was further discussed at a corporate retreat in January 2000 involving some 170 people. Representatives from several key partners in aftercare (SCORE, Industrial and Services Co-operative Society, Singapore Aftercare Association and Singapore Anti-Narcotic Association) and the Ministry also joined prison officers at the retreat. This corporate retreat helped the task force and the leadership team to co-create and crystallise the blueprint for the future of the Prison Service. The different projects in the matrix of vision markers versus functions (Annex 8.1) were linked and grouped to produce four focal areas. For each focal area, several anchor projects were identified. These were priority projects that would be implemented in the next three years and the other projects identified in the matrix would be delegated to subordinate units to drive (for example, the Prison School project was by then well under way and it was delegated to the Prison School to continue with its development) or be kept in view for future implementation. The key levers were resources common to the projects that needed to be developed to help us do more with less in implementation. This blueprint would be reviewed every three years and was as follows:

Focal Area 1: Enhancing Operational Capabilities (five anchor projects)

- HUMANS
- Outsourcing
- Contingency & Emergency Planning
- Zero tolerance policy against gangs
- Changi Prison Complex Redevelopment

Focal Area 2: Staff Development (three anchor projects)

- Staff Ethics Structure & Code of Ethics
- Selection tools & definition of quality staff
- Staff development, training, welfare and retention of staff

Focal Area 3: Integrated Incare (three anchor projects)

- Integrated Classification System
- Programme Integration & Development
- Prison Management System Rehab Module

Focal Area 4: Co-ordinated Aftercare (four anchor projects)

- CARE Network
- Tail-end Home Detention
- Absorption of SCORE Counselling Centre
- Family involvement

The three key levers were technology, knowledge management and community resources.

This blueprint was presented at the work plan seminar 2000 and another corporate retreat was organised in June 2000 to firm up implementation. For the first time in our journey, we had a major reality check. Up to this point, when everyone was talking in terms of the corporate future, all was excitement and creative tension. As soon as we started talking about the actual work, the enormity of the tasks involved suddenly overwhelmed everyone that would have a part in the blueprint and the balloon popped. The energy that was unleashed during the visioning was nowhere to be seen. As the leader, I had to insist that no one would be allowed to leave during the 3-day retreat until we produced an action plan for each anchor project, with agreed timelines and targets. This was a particularly trying retreat and it would have been a failure without my insistence on results. On the third day, we finally finished the implementation plan on a giant whiteboard and I asked all the project leaders to take a photo together in front of the board. This photo would later be used to remind the key officers of the commitment they made that day. After all had been said and done, the gathering broke out into spontaneous celebration. The pathways to the future of the Prison Service had finally become clear!

Annex 8.1   Strategising Framework*

Vision Mission	Staff	Family	Community	Criminal Justice System
Security	i) HUMANS ii) CPC-PMS iii) Quality of staff iv) Anti-graft strategy v) Cps Development vi) Organisational & Staff Development vii) Intel network and security/intel mindset viii) Internal Communication ix) Build Up Logistics Branch's Capability x) Leverage on Technology	i) Anti-graft strategy ii) A formalised structure to facilitate interaction & feedback between staff and inmates' families (e.g. for PS, counsellors, intel officers, form an association, etc.) iii) CPC-PMS iv) Review of visit items v) External Communication vi) Leverage on Technology	i) Intel network and mindset (e.g. in religious counsellors, HWHs, SACA, SANA, etc.) ii) Community policing (e.g. during escapes, fires, etc.) iii) Security training for volunteers iv) Education of Community & Media Co-operation v) Leverage on Technology	i) Intel network / sharing ii) Educating CJS iii) Appropriate sentencing iv) Information sharing with judiciary on inmates and staff v) Image building vi) Leverage on Technology
Rehabilitation	i) Quality of staff ii) Staff Posting iii) HUMANS	i) Family Service Centre & Services	i) Revisiting the role and function of NCADA	i) Sharing of Information with Probation Services, Juvenile Courts, etc.

(Continued)

*For list of abbreviations used in Chapter 8, refer to Annex 8.2.

Annex 8.1 (Continued)

Vision Mission	Staff	Family	Community	Criminal Justice System
	iv) CPC-PMS v) Structure and system to operate the throughcare concept vi) Specialist and structured programme development vii) Develop capabilities to monitor, evaluate and maintain programme integrity viii) Internal Industrial Division ix) Social force x) Intel network & culture xi) Internal Communication xii) Leverage on Technology	ii) Sharing of route map with family members, charting with their inputs iii) Linking inmates' families to resources from their own communities iv) Leverage on Technology	ii) Local and national initiative spearheaded by SACA. iii) Involvement of community in incare activities iv) Community Education & Media Co-operation v) Intel network & mindset vi) Leverage on Technology	ii) Appropriate sentencing iii) Educating CJS iv) Enforcement agencies giving deterrent talks in prisons v) Research vi) Restorative Justice vii) External Communication viii) Integration of efforts
Prevention	i) Preventive education for inmates and family members (e.g. PDE, Prison visits)	i) Family Support Groups	i) Working with Crime Prevention Council	i) Research (predictive angle that will hit all 16 boxes)

(Continued)

Annex 8.1 (*Continued*)

Vision Mission	Staff	Family	Community	Criminal Justice System
	ii) Intel network & mindset iii) More active partnership in existing prevention programmes by Prisons (e.g. OSY, etc.) iv) Build Research Capability v) Social force vi) Internal Communication	ii) Association to run parenting programmes, work with FSCs iii) Research to support iv) Feedback network v) Leverage on Technology	ii) Research iii) Intel network/ mindset iv) Community Education & Media Co-operation vi) Leverage on Technology	ii) Intel network/ mindset iii) External Communication iv) Leverage on Technology
Aftercare	i) Job placement for released offenders (SCORE's JPU) ii) Integration and strengthening the aftercare network iii) HUMANS iv) Internal Communication v) Leverage on Technology	i) Family Education ii) Support groups for family members to sustain them iii) Leverage on Technology for Aftercare	i) Building community acceptance and non-rejection, e.g. future employers, schools for inmates' upgrading, etc. ii) Mobilising the NGOs iii) Education & Media Co-operation iv) Reformed Ex-offenders Association v) Intel network/mindset vi) Leverage on Technology	i) Supervision of Re-leased Offenders ii) Feedback to Courts and LEAs (close the loop) iii) Changing mental models of enforce-ment agencies iv) Intel network/ mindset v) Leverage on Technology

For example, Box "Security–Staff" indicates staff's contribution towards security, Box "Security-Family" indicates family's contribution towards security, Box "Rehabilitation-Criminal Justice System" indicates what CJS can contribute to rehabilitation, etc.

Notes on Strategising Framework

Security

Secure custody refers to ensuring that offenders are securely detained, adequately housed, clothed, fed and humanely treated. Secure custody will remain as a pre-requisite which must be met before there can be rehabilitation.

Rehabilitation

Rehabilitation refers to the programmes and opportunities to meet the unique needs of the various types of offenders so that we release a " rehabilitated offender" who not only has a smaller chance of re-offending and harming society and citizens but is also a better person. These programmes can assist them in becoming not only better prisoners during their incarceration but also changing their criminal behaviour and enhancing their potential for successful re-integration with the community.

Prevention

Prevention refers to the activities in two broad categories:

a) Preventing the general public or potential offenders from offending
b) Preventing re-offending (i.e. commission of institutional offences) of offenders in prisons

Aftercare

Aftercare refers to the care given to the prisoner or drug addict after he has been released from the Prisons. Once released, offenders must continue to be provided with programmes, support and supervision to help them sustain the positive change they have benefited from during incare.

Staff

Individual staff and Prisons as a whole
Inclusive of SCORE

Family

Inmates' families

Community

Prisons' neighbours
The community of the offenders: CDC
Strategic partners in rehabilitation: SACA, SANA, ISCOS, NCADA, Employers, HWHs, VWOs, other helping agencies
Media Corporation
Greater community

CJS

Judiciary: Sub-Courts, High Courts, Juvenile Courts, Family Courts
Attorney-General's Chambers: Civil Division and Criminal Section
Enforcement Agencies: Police, CNB, SIR, CPIB, ISD, CED
Social Agencies: MCD, Probation Services, Homes, Detention Barracks

Annex 8.2: Notes on Abbreviations in Chapter 8

CDC	— Community Development Council
CED	— Customs Enforcement Division
CJS	— Criminal Justice System
CNB	— Central Narcotics Bureau
CPC-PMS	— Changi Prison Complex — Prison Management System
CPIB	— Corrupt Practices Investigation Bureau
CARE	— Community Action for the Rehabilitation of Ex-Offenders
FSC	— Family Service Centre
HUMANS	— Housing Unit Management System
HWH	— Half-way House
ISCOS	— Industrial and Services Co-operative Society
ISD	— Internal Security Department
JPU	— Job Placement Unit
MCD	— Ministry of Community Development
NCADA	— National Council Against Drug Abuse
NGO	— Non-government Organisation
OSY	— Out-of-school Youth
PDE	— Preventive Drug Education
SACA	— Singapore Aftercare Association
SANA	— Singapore Anti-Narcotic Association
SCORE	— Singapore Corporation of Rehabilitative Enterprises
SIR	— Singapore Immigration & Registration Department
VWO	— Volunteer Welfare Organisation

CHAPTER NINE

THE FIRST INITIATIVES

It is apparent from this list of 15 anchor projects that a great many initiatives had already started before we got to this point. Many of these initiatives were internal to the Prison Service and aimed at making the service more efficient, more focused and more aligned to the vision. I will just deal with one such initiative here, namely the ethics structure. In Chapters 2 and 3, where I touched on the origin of HUMANS, I mentioned the fact that there had been cases of prison officers being compromised by inmates. When we started to experiment with HUMANS, we were well aware that this problem might re-surface if we did not have a way to deal with the ethical dilemmas that a prison officer would inevitably face when he became familiar with his charges. How should he deal with the hard luck stories that inmates would come up with from time to time to seek his help beyond what was allowed? To an officer new to the service, this would be emotionally draining. We need to give him all the support possible to make the judgement call and if, indeed, some interventions beyond the rules were called for, we should re-examine the rules. What we must not do was to treat every hard luck story as an attempt to compromise our officer and reject it out of hand. The result of this line of thought resulted in the ethics structure.

The first element of the ethics structure was a comprehensive code of ethics to deal with the normal hard luck stories. It would codify past wisdom of dealing with such cases and provide a practical guide to Prison Officers on what to do. It would be a living document which continually captures new experiences and wisdom. When the situation that surfaced was not in the code of ethics, then the problem would be brought to an "ethics circle" comprising more senior and experienced officers for deliberation. The structure mandated that the circles had to meet regularly. If a problem was urgent in nature and occurred in between the regular meetings, then an "ethics officer" who was in charge of the ethics structure in the unit would be immediately accessible to the officers concerned to provide quick advice. With such a structure, no officer had any excuse to take his own action and become compromised. The anchor project would require the development of the code of ethics and standard operating procedures for the entire structure.

Two of the anchor projects that were not internal to the Prison Service would later prove to be pivotal in its reform: the CARE Network and the family involvement project. Family involvement was first experimented in the Prison School. I will deal with family involvement in greater detail later as the subject did not have an immediate impact this point. I will deal with the CARE Network here. Given our vision statement which says that we must work with the community, I went about surveying the landscape of the aftercare services available and then got all the players together to co-ordinate their efforts. The CARE Network could thus be described as a gathering of aftercare agencies that were willing to subject themselves to co-ordination. It was offi-cially formed in May 2000.

At first, I did not intend to put myself forward to chair the CARE Network, which I described as a gathering of players in the field of aftercare, voluntarily subjecting themselves to being co-ordinated. I wanted my friend and the Chairman of the SCORE board, Kong Mun Kwong to play the role. An emi-nent citizen, a Justice of the Peace and a respected business-man, his leadership role in the SCORE board also gave him the license to provide leadership to the CARE Network. However, Mun Kwong persuaded me that since the Prison Service was the only agency that could refer released prison inmates to the aftercare agencies, only the Prison Service would be able to hold the group together and therefore, I had to occupy the chair. Eventually, we agreed on a compromise to co-chair the group. The Prison Service and SCORE would also form a joint secretariat to the CARE Network.

The Programme Branch, which was formed under the Operations Division to spearhead the implementation and development of rehabilitation programmes, would also take on the key support role to the CARE Network. The first head of Programme Branch was Ms Lee Kwai Sem, whose industry, patience and doggedness made her the perfect choice for the role of heading the Secretariat of the CARE Network. Professor Ho Peng Kee, our champion in the Ministry, officiated at the official launch of the CARE Net-work. The Programme Branch would eventually have more than 100 trained social workers, known as counsellors in its fold. Under my successor, it was finally upgraded to a full division. What my predecessor had sought was finally achieved by my successor.

Gathering the agencies together was one thing, but getting them to act in concert was quite another. Eventually, what made the CARE Network tick was the new Case Management Framework with the government providing 90% of the funding on a per case basis. In truth, the government did not provide any new money. The Prison Service had to cough up more than half of the money needed from its baseline budget. We also persuaded SCORE and the National Council for Social Service (NCSS) which is the agency set up to support efforts in social service in Singapore, to chip in. With the then CEO of SCORE retiring in early 2002, I managed to persuade the Ministry as well as Mun Kwong that the CEO of SCORE should henceforth be a Prison Officer. This would not only ensure that SCORE would be aligned with the vision of the Prison Service, it would also bring about mutual understanding on the needs of the respective organisations. The first Prison Officer chosen to take up the post was Jason Wong. With this connection in place, SCORE would eventually play a key role in the Yellow Ribbon Project which I will touch on later.

Over the years, we continued to refine the corporate planning process as we gained more experience and confidence about the methodology we adopted. We were to decide later that 11 anchor projects were far too many for the service to cope with. We found that once a project was chosen as an anchor project, R&P, being the driver of the work plan, would pressurise the project leaders to drive action. The project leaders would in turn drive the ground hard to ensure fast-track implementation. The amount of stress on the ground would become quite overwhelming. In later years, we still used the same method to review the gaps between the current reality and the end-state as articulated in the vision statement. However, after the project list was agreed on, we would use a democratic vote to choose three anchor projects to focus on at any one time. In the first year after the vision statement was crafted, the ground officers were driven to distraction in our zeal to get things done. Nevertheless, looking back, I would not say that it was a mistake. Without the initial push to generate momentum, we would not have achieved so much in such a short time. Unfortunately, the stress put on the organisation would subsequently emerge in a manner that caused us much anguish.

The other lesson I learned in this process was that just because we decided on the projects based on our belief that they would bring us nearer to the vision, it did not mean that they would actually do so. We need to review them regularly and fine tune their implementations. When they clearly did not work, we need to have the courage to abandon them. The other key lesson is that, the vision should define the end-state as broadly as possible so that it can last the test of time. At a new stage of development, the vision needs to be re-visited not necessarily for the vision statement to be revised, but more for the new understanding brought about by experience to be incorporated into a new understanding of the vision.

CHAPTER TEN

OVERCOMING RESISTANCE FROM WITHIN

By the end of 1999, I could look back with some satisfaction at the strides that we had made to embrace the idea of rehabilitation. For one, we had our vision and mission statement but second, and more importantly, a lot had been accomplished on the ground: the Prison School had opened its doors; R&P (Research and Planning branch) and Programme Branch had been set up and the rehabilitation framework was in place; HUMANS was beginning to be accepted as the right model for inmate management; and the strategy for the next three years had been forged and it would be presented at the Work Plan Seminar in May. A few other things had also been accomplished. I managed to strengthen our intelligence capability by borrowing two Police intelligence officers from the Police for the Prison Intelligence Branch. I had also borrowed officers from the Civil Defence Force to strengthen our Operations Division and Logistics Branch. Everything appeared set for take-off.

However, I had one major worry. The entire visioning exercise had involved some 700 officers, about a third of our staff strength, but the other two thirds had not been directly engaged by the leadership team. I also thought that the intervention of the Ministry in the visioning process had one possible undesirable consequence — it might have diluted the commitment to rehabilitation. I had heard rumblings on the ground that security would be the Prison Service's eternal focus and rehabilitation was only the flavour of the current director. I therefore wanted to assess the ground sentiment to see if the quick wins we had achieved had managed to tip the balance in favour of the current administration's approach. In order to answer this question, I asked R&P to conduct an Organisational Climate Survey as well as to organise some focus groups to explore the issues involved in greater depth.

It was Shie Yong Lee who presented the results of the survey to the leadership team. The survey indicated that the move to embrace rehabilitation did not enjoy popular support and indeed, the majority believed that the moment I left my post, the entire rehabilitation movement would collapse. Many officers thought that the management operated in an ivory tower, without understanding the difficulty ground officers faced while managing inmates. The feedback that riled me the most was that some officers thought too much had been done for inmates and too little for the staff. Yong Lee was in tears when many of the leadership team members expressed shock and dismay at the results as she struggled to defend the findings. I could sense discouragement and negative sentiment in the room, as if we were ready to give up because of one negative report. I knew I had to weigh in.

I told the meeting that we should accept the findings and move on. As far as I was concerned, if we believed what we were doing was right, then no amount of resistance was going to stop us. I also told the meeting that I believed in the critical mass principle. Since we had engaged almost a third of our staff in co-creating the vision, there must be a certain level of support. Indeed, this was also borne out by the survey results. We could move on with the support of this critical mass and in time, the main body of staff would come around.

We went on to deliberate on how we should deal with the findings and I opined that we should present the findings at the Work Plan Seminar and grab the bull by the horns. It would also give me an opportunity to tell the audience that I would not be going away any time soon. If rehabilitation was my flavour, then I would hang around long enough to see to it that the flavour would become part of the DNA of the Prison Service.

The Work Plan Seminar 2000 went off well. The main theme of the seminar was to inject passion into our work in line with the vision. The R&P staff did a good job in presenting the strategy for the next three years and made the whole occasion uplifting. At the end, after the findings of the survey were presented, I availed myself to be interviewed by a former TV presenter, who also happened to be an ex-offender, in a segment called "In Conversation" (named after a TV programme the presenter used to anchor). I was able to deal with questions from the floor and made the pitch that I had planned for. However, I was under no illusion that the resistance would just go away. It would re-surface from time to time and at almost every Work Plan Seminar thereafter, the debate on security versus rehabilitation would recur. My worry was proven true. By diluting the commitment to rehabilitation in our vision statement, the Ministry had unwittingly entrenched the "security" camp in the Prison Service. In truth, security in the prisons is fundamental to any rehabilitative efforts. If prisoners do not feel safe, it is impossible to run any meaningful rehabilitation programmes. However, the reflexes on the ground had been against rehabilitation because they thought that it would compromise security. It was that same old mindset that stopped us from employing inmate clerks before I came on the scene. I intended that the vision statement should once and for all remove that mindset. However, that was not to be even after my tenure of nine years.

The Work Plan Seminar also showed me another fact that I had not seen clearly until then. In my initial months as the Director, I had met many idealistic young men and women who joined the service to help others. I realised that this was by no means universal. The questions many officers asked me at the Work Plan Seminar showed me that they were self-serving and short-sighted. I was not dealing with a bunch of altruistic do-gooders. They were as human as the average man on the street.

I decided then and there that I had to do one more thing. I had to gather those idealistic young men and women in a retreat to fortify them before they too succumbed to their human instinct of self before all else. I must explain to them my innermost motivation to do what I was about to embark on and share with them my dreams and fears. I must extend their horizons far into the future where they would find themselves in so that they would stay the course prescribed by the vision statement. I decided to call the retreat a scenario planning retreat although we would not be doing much scenario planning. At the beginning of the retreat, I gave the group a speech that explained it all. I can do no better than attaching the speech in Annex 10.1 to this chapter.

Annex 10.1: Opening Speech at Scenario Planning Retreat (12–13 October 2000)

Introduction

Before I go into the details of what we are going to deal with at this retreat, I must tell you that this retreat is your retreat. I am here as your advisor, consultant, a provocateur to get you to think beyond your current situation. Today and tomorrow, you will be discussing, talking and debating about a future which I will not be in. Look around the room, there is no one beyond the age of 40 other than the Deputy Director and me. The future we are talking about is in 15 to 20 years time. It is your retreat because it is your future.

During this retreat, we will be talking about future scenarios that will be radically different from what we have today. I will elaborate more on this later. I do not see the need to stress out and alarm many of our more junior officers by getting the entire service involved in this exercise. For many of our officers, they are contented to just focus on their job at hand. The 3-year strategic framework and anchor projects have already generated much stress or perceived stress, or so I was told. I have decided that as long as the leaders of the service are clear about the longer term future and keep the longer term agenda constantly in mind, we need not burden the masses.

Earlier Visioning Exercise

I feel that the problem with the earlier visioning exercise was its public nature and objectives. It was more of a show of commitment for an internal audience and an external audience. It was done with our heads more than our hearts.

The current vision statement is to me a mere pendulum swing in our thinking, from focusing on security to rehabilitation. There is no major breakthrough in thinking. We are still hemmed in by our old custodial mindset that is very much grounded in operational work and safe custody of prisoners. Nevertheless, there is no turning back from what we had already decided, given the investment of political capital on the vision. A vision does not stand for all time and it needs constant re-interpretation to stay relevant. While we may not want to change the vision statement too frequently, we must be able to re-interpret it as we move on and when the landscape looks different.

Epochal Changes

The questions that we should ask ourselves are: how can we add value to society? What can we do if we do not have prisoners to look after? This is an important element that is lacking in the current vision, as it did not take into consideration possible epochal changes which will affect the development of the service. For example, back in history, the invention of paper enabled the codification of knowledge; the invention of the printing press revolutionised the spread of knowledge and the invention of steam engine increased the mobility of human capital.

Right now, the world is in the process of going through a new epochal change with the development of the internet and its related information and communication technologies that have grown faster than any other technology in history. Interactive cyberspace has become a new medium for civilisation and is evolving into a global brain and nervous system for humanity. This epochal change would become more apparent in the next 10 years or so to the men on the street.

The Prison Service would have to attempt to make sense of her role and purpose in this fast-changing environment and gear itself up for certain inevitabilities. We will not be shielded from the larger driving forces and developments in our society and the world. Some of these developments are trends that we can watch out for and be prepared to respond to. Others are uncertain and unpredictable. A new technology or paradigm may render some of our work instantly obsolete or irrelevant. One inevitable result of new technology will be that information will move at the speed of light at a mouse-click. It will drastically reduce our response time to events and situations and people will expect instant answers to their questions.

First World

Singapore cannot hope to be a first world country and not follow first world rules on how society should be organised. You can see that our society is increasingly influenced by international standards. This has been especially so in the last few years. In the law and order arena, we have resisted this turn of the tide for a long time. This cannot be sustained. We will continue to lose our "powers". We will need to find other ways to manage and get our work done within the rules of the first world. This is not going soft! It is being realistic and practical. Many of our officers will have a hard time understanding this. It will get harder and harder to deliver on our work as our previous convenient but less than transparent practices give way to more transparent ones. The new adjudication procedure is an example of anticipating possible future problems and taking corrective measures now. We have no choice however long we resist the change.

In 20 years, we will operate very differently from now. The impact of the ascendance of the Western model of liberal democracy and human rights on our society cannot be underestimated. This encroachment of the western liberal ideology could change the face of politics in Singapore and impinge on our current practices, such as caning, hanging and detention without trial.

Changes in Political and Judicial Leadership

In 20 years, many current leaders in this country who shaped our systemic structures and institutions, advocated and supported the existing mental models will no longer be around.

In 20 years, western liberal democratic thinking will have made major inroads into our society. The political and social climate will evolve very differently when younger leaders take over. We are beginning to see this happening. The Speakers' Corner is a good example. It was unthinkable a few years ago. The liberalisation of our economy and the opening up of our telecom markets are other examples of changing mental models in government.

What Does the Prison Service Ultimately Want to Work For?

The time is now ripe to envision the longer-term horizon. As the Service works out its three-year plan, you must ask yourself whether you want to be a "player" in the future or merely be content to react to events as they unfold. To be a "player" is to chart your own destination with your specific rationale, passion and agenda. Not to be one means we will continue to be shaped by other people's agenda and ideas.

This retreat will, I hope, enable us to think about these important issues. It will not be the final word on this matter. Rather, I hope that by bringing you together and throwing some of these issues at you, I have started a process of what I call "strategic thinking" among you.

As such, this retreat is the real visioning exercise. It is not really meant for us to do scenario planning *per se*. We are here not to forecast the future, but to anticipate plausible developments and decide on our responses should they arise. "How can we add value to society?" will be a question we will constantly ask ourselves in this retreat. I hope to hear more in-depth thinking on the following questions that I would be posing for your breakout group discussions.

Objectives We Hope to Achieve at the Retreat

The following questions have been weighing on my heart for many nights. Questions 1 & 2 would be tackled on day 1 while question 3 would be addressed on day 2:

Q1 How can the Prison Service add value to society given our intellectual capital, expertise, stature, etc. and a 20-year time frame?

Q2 What other capabilities must we develop in order to add value to society?
Helping question: Is there something beyond locking up and rehabilitating inmates?

Q3 How do we bring about this long-term vision?

Helping question: What is the range of scenarios and our responses?

Before all of you break out for your group discussions, I would like to summarise my own views on these questions for all of you to chew on.

First of all, we must break the custody mindset. The Changi Prison Complex (CPC) should not be the source of pride that it is today. We should not be proud of the fact that we are locking up a large number of our citizens. One of the things I have come across in my readings is that sometimes it goes beyond destroying outmoded mindset in order to change things. We may have to destroy physical assets as well! Think about it in relation to the CPC. We must aim to have as few people locked up as possible. I am not saying that wrongdoers should go unpunished. Rather, we should look beyond imprisonment into other means of punishment and extracting "our pound of flesh".

We must break loose from the bureaucratic framework that we are locked in today. If we are to have any chance of making reforms to our system, we should aim to be a body that can set our own direction and carry out our mission based on our convictions and our beliefs. We therefore must influence policy-making in crime and punishment much more than now. We must always have our long term goal of having as few people locked up as possible at the back of our mind when we respond to policies on crime and punishment.

We must move up the society's value-chain and garner greater emotional investment from society toward our work. We must be seen by society as contributing to its betterment rather than just a holding centre for its unwanted elements. We must become a social institution that is needed as well as wanted by society.

The Future Depends on You

To achieve the outcome we want, we must decide on the strategies we need to follow. We will need to know what the drivers are that will determine the success of our strategies. We will have to realistically assess whether we are capable of carrying out the strategies and if not, what capabilities we need to build up to do so.

I strongly believe that whether the Prison Service can succeed will largely depend on the quality of thinking of our people. Today, we will take one more step toward improving our quality of thinking together.

CHAPTER ELEVEN

CORPORATE IMAGE CAMPAIGN

One of the many threads of thinking that came out of the scenario planning retreat was the importance of creating the correct corporate image for the Prison Service. I always believe that advertising only works if one has a good product or a good idea to sell. Especially in this electronic age, what we are and what we do becomes public knowledge very quickly. If we try to paint ourselves as someone better than we are, we will soon be found out and be branded hypocrites and cheats instead of being associated with the desired corporate image. I also believe that advertising is not just for external audiences. More importantly, it is for the internal audience as well. It is a signal that we are prepared to back up what we are trying to achieve internally with a public message. Although a corporate image campaign was always at the back of my mind to help change the public perception about the Prison Service, I had to wait for the right moment to do so. I had to be confident that we had enough substance to go public about our new emphasis on helping inmates to become useful citizens. By substance, I did not just mean the systemic structures we had put in place to effect the change, but also the change in organisational culture to support such an approach.

Following the Work Plan Seminar 2000, we did a second Organisational Climate Survey to see whether the Seminar had the desired effect on the ground using by and large the same questionnaire as the first survey. This time, the results were much more encouraging. It showed that 80% of our officers agreed with the new vision and mission statements and believed that we could fulfil them. What difference a few months had made! Judging from the survey, the Prison Service had begun to take on a new corporate identity, accepting the new set of values and principles that would drive their work from henceforth. I thought it was time to forge a new corporate image to project this new corporate identity. The aim was not just to communicate what the service wanted to achieve, but also to garner public acceptance and support for the change as well as to attract people who could identify themselves with our corporate identity to join the service. Following the Ministry's approval for the project, a public relations firm, Burson Masteller was appointed as our consultant for the corporate image campaign and it, in turn, brought in the advertising firm Dentsu Young to be in charge of the creative aspects of the project.

The brief given to the creative team was to project a corporate image that comprised four elements. Firstly, the Prison Service sought to rehabilitate offenders and was effective in this work. Secondly, the Prison Service protected society by keeping offenders in secure custody. Thirdly, the Prison Service was a "New Economy" organisation that valued organisational learning, knowledge creation and innovation. Fourthly, the Prison Service was a professional organisation run by professional officers.

The consultants planned a series of activities and events to carry out the advertising campaign. At the core the campaign was three television commercials (TVCs) that cleverly encapsulated the four elements of the new corporate image and introduced the tagline: "Captains of lives; rehab, renew, restart."

The first TVC was titled "Tattoo". It opened with a scruffy character sharpening a knife intently and this was spliced with scenes of loud diners feasting in a restaurant. With ominous music in the background, the set-up created the impression that the character was about to attack someone in the restaurant, probably the waitress who just turned her back to the camera. The impression was then quickly dispelled when the camera zoomed out to reveal that the subject was a chef in the restaurant's kitchen carving a water melon. At this point, the discerning viewers would realise that with her cheongsam, the lower back of the waitress looked exactly like a water melon. The TVC then ended with the voice-over: "Who says ex-convicts can't serve society with conviction."

The second TVC was titled "Circuit Board". It opened with snippets of prison scenes: a watch-tower, barbed wire fences, a closed circuit camera and a warning sign. The scenes were shot in a dull and dark fashion to suggest that something bad was afoot. We then saw a prisoner in close up trying to undo something on a circuit board with a screwdriver. It appeared that he had managed to short-circuit the security system as a prison gate opened. The twist was delivered when an officer walked through the gate into the computer assembly workshop where the prisoner was. The prisoner was merely hard at work assembling a computer. The voice-over then said: "We believe, with rehabilitation, doing time is not a waste of time."

The third TVC, titled "Witness", was to me the most telling of all. It showed how quickly a person could jump to conclusions because of his or her bias and prejudice. In this TVC, a lady driver spots a little girl sitting all by herself on a street bench through the rear-view mirror of her parked car. A scruffy man, with tattoos all over, approaches the girl. He starts talking to the girl and finally pulls her along to go somewhere. The lady driver becomes worried, seeming ready to come to the rescue of the girl. The camera then reveals the pair being joined by a lady who is apparently the mother of the girl and the three walk off happily hand in hand. The lady driver smiles with relief as she realised how wrong she was. The voice-over then said: "Whilst it's easy to see the flaws in people, it's also important to see the good in them."

The corporate image campaign was implemented at the end of 2001. It generated tremendous resonance and, with hindsight, it is fair to say that it achieved all the intended objectives and more. In fact, the resonance from within was the loudest of all. Many Prison Officers told me that the campaign had uplifted their spirits and self-esteem. From that time on, more Prison Officers proudly told their friends that they worked for the Prison Service when previously, they were coy about doing so. From 2002 onwards, the difficulty in recruitment experienced by the Service became a thing of the past. The new corporate identity "Captains of lives: rehab, renew, restart", communicated through the corporate image campaign, had woven its magic. With even more bright and idealistic young people joining us and ready to throw themselves into the work of rehabilitation, the transformation of the Prison Service gathered momentum.

By the beginning of 2002 when the corporate image campaign of the Prison Service was underway in earnest,

Chapter Eleven

SCORE (Singapore Corporation of Rehabilitative Enterprises) too was forging its new corporate identity. By then, Jason Wong had become the CEO of SCORE. Both Jason and Mun Kwong were keenly aware that unless SCORE stepped up and played its part in rehabilitation, it would be in danger of becoming irrelevant. SCORE held a corporate retreat to address the issues involved and brought the organisation into alignment with the vision and mission of the Prison Service. Following the retreat, SCORE adopted new vision and mission statements too. Its mission statement stated: "We rehabilitate and help reintegrate offenders to become responsible and contributing members of society." Its vision statement stated: "We build bridges of hope for offenders and their families. We contribute to a safer community by successfully reintegrating offenders. We exemplify and lead in creating a more compassionate society that offers second chances." To encapsulate its ambition, it adopted the tagline "Building bridges. Changing lives."

Following this, the Prison Service and SCORE took a few simple but highly symbolic moves to cement the alliance. The Prison Service and SCORE signed a Memorandum of Understanding (MOU) to jointly pledge commitment to the work of rehabilitation and reintegration, and the SCORE headquarters moved into the same premises as the Prison headquarters. From that point on, the two organisations would stand shoulder to shoulder in their common quest of helping ex-offenders become useful citizens. In an indirect way, the corporate image campaign had precipitated the alliance between the Prison Service and SCORE. The campaign accentuated the corporate identity of the Prison Service and made it quite obvious that SCORE needed to change too if they were to keep up.

CHAPTER TWELVE

YELLOW RIBBON PROJECT

The newly minted alliance between the Prison Service and SCORE did not come a moment too soon. With the success of the corporate image campaign focussing on building a new corporate identity for the Prison Service, it was now time to broaden the public relations campaign to garner public support for aftercare of ex-offenders. The need to do this was patently obvious. No matter how well the Prison Service did to rehabilitate offenders; the time would come when they would be released back to society. The real world challenge for them would be of a different order than the controlled world of prison. They needed the support and understanding of their family, friends, prospective employers and the community around them to give them another chance to make good. I decided to ask SCORE to spearhead this effort because SCORE played a key role in promoting the employment of ex-offenders in the community. To broaden the support base, I believed it was a good idea to present this new campaign as a CARE Network initiative. CARE Network was after all about aftercare.

It then fell upon Jason Wong to conceptualise the campaign. It was fortuitous that a Prison Officer happened to come across a performance of the song "Tie a Yellow Ribbon around the Old Oak Tree" and realised that the song was about a prisoner returning home after being released from prison. This was brought to the attention of Jason. Further research revealed that the song was based on an actual incident in US. The central character had been released from prison after serving a 3-year sentence for passing bad checks. He was bound for his home town and had explained to the driver that he had written to his wife telling her she did not have to wait for him. However, he had asked his wife to signify her forgiveness by tying a yellow ribbon around the only oak tree in the city square of White Oak, Georgia. As the bus approached the town, the driver slowed down to check the oak tree. Sure enough, there was a yellow ribbon there. The key lines in the song that inspired Jason were: "I'm really still in prison and my love, she still holds the key. A simple yellow ribbon's what I need to set me free." These lines aptly describe an ex-offender's need for acceptance and forgiveness from his loved ones and the community in order to set him free from the prison within him, what we later dubbed the second prison.

When the idea of using a yellow ribbon to symbolise the need for ex-offenders to be given second chances was first presented by Jason, it did not meet with immediate popular support. Our PR consultants thought it would be difficult to persuade men to wear a yellow ribbon to signify their support for the cause because it might appear a feminine thing to do. Others pointed out that the yellow ribbon had been adopted to represent other causes, like veterans returning home in the US. Some also felt that the song in question was such an old song that it would not resonate with many people.

However, I thought the idea was a novel one and supported it whole-heartedly. I also contributed funding to the project from the baseline budget of the Prison Service. When the concept was presented to the CARE Network, member organisations too threw their support behind the idea and agreed to play their parts in the campaign. The basic construct for the campaign was, at an appointed period every year; yellow ribbons would be peddled on the streets and malls for a small donation. Wearing the ribbon would signify a person's support for the cause of giving ex-offenders second chances. During the period, events both within and outside the prisons would be planned to promote the cause. As part of the project, the CARE Network also agreed to set up a fund by tapping on public donations, to be known as the Yellow Ribbon Fund. It would be used to fund three principal rehabilitative services: first, to assist ex-offenders to normalise their lives after they are released from prison; second, to support awareness programmes aimed at creating awareness and inspiring community action for the rehabilitation and reintegration of ex-offenders and third, to assist family members of prisoners before and after their discharge from custody.

The first Chairman of the committee overseeing the fund was my predecessor Mr Poh Geok Ek who had by then become the President of the Singapore Anti-Narcotic Association (SANA) with Mr Phillip Tan, a visiting Justice and the Treasurer of the National Council for Social Service (NCSS) as the vice chairman. Later, Phillip, an innovative fund raiser, would take over the chair and under him, the Yellow Ribbon Fund managed to raise about a million dollars a year to fund assistance schemes for inmates, inmates' family and ex-offenders.

The first year of the Yellow Ribbon Project (2004) marked the beginning of many interesting annual activities and events. A song-writing competition was held among serving prison inmates and the prize for the winners was an opportunity to perform the songs they had written before their family members. This proved to be a great hit. Subsequently, the same idea was expanded to include a cooking competition and a poetry writing competition. Prison inmates now keenly looked forward to these annual events so that they could perform or cook for their family members should they be numbered among the winners. It was a moving experience to be present when the inmates were awarded their prizes. Their families would be invited to attend and it gave them the opportunity to appreciate firsthand the progress their loved one had made on the path of recovery. The prize winners would take the opportunity to speak of their remorse and apologise to their families for causing them much pain through their follies that landed them in prison. Many tears were shed and many reconciliations took place at such gatherings.

One spin-off from the cooking competition was a programme called "Dining Behind Bars". The idea of the cooking competition came from the food-loving Mum Kwong who was himself an accomplished chef. He also realised that food could be used to raise funds for the Yellow Ribbon Fund. The award winning inmate chefs would cook for those who joined in "Dining Behind Bars" costing $200 per person. This was typically held once a month on a Saturday. As part of the package, these visitors would first be given a tour of the prison facilities before sitting down to lunch. The programme attracted many companies, groups and individuals who would not normally have a chance to visit prisons. The quality of food, the prison facilities and rehabilitation efforts regularly impressed the visitors and gained the Yellow Ribbon Project many supporters. Later, at Phillip Tan's suggestion, an auction of inmates's art was added to the programme, which raised more funds for the Yellow Ribbon Fund.

Another annual event which started under the banner of the Yellow Ribbon Project was the annual prison open-house. Members of the public could visit the prisons to see what prison conditions were like and be entertained by prisoners either through performances or art and craft exhibitions. Other public events organised over the years included public concerts performed by prison inmates, the community art exhibition, the Yellow Ribbon Big Walk and, subsequently, the Yellow Ribbon Run. At every such event, the galvanising symbol was the yellow ribbon. Ribbons were worn by participants and prominently displayed in interesting ways at event sites or along event routes. The presence of celebrities and political leaders such as the President, the Prime Minister and other Ministers and members of Parliament further enhanced the profile and visibility of the campaign. The campaign also succeeded in mobilising support among religious organisations to accept released prisoners into their fold. More employers became aware of ex-offenders' plight in finding jobs and came forward to offer their help. In time, an alliance of sorts among employers was built up to support the employment of ex-offenders in aftercare.

In the inaugural year of 2004, the Yellow Ribbon Project was anchored by a charity concert performed almost entirely by serving inmates. The presence of the President of the Republic of Singapore gave the project a dream beginning. Some 5000 people packed the Singapore Indoor Stadium to share an evening with serving and former prisoners. At a poignant moment of the concert, the emcee asked all of those in the audience who had served prison terms to stand up and identify themselves. I was surprised at the number of people who stood up and the rousing applause they received, many in tears. I never imagined something like that could have happened in a conservative society like Singapore. From that moment, I realised that we had started something big, something that would make Singapore a different society. The other important fact about the concert was that it was organised almost entirely by volunteers. It set the scene for future years when volunteers became the real heroes behind the success of the Yellow Ribbon Project. It gave rise to a social movement that is still going strong this day.

The success of the Yellow Ribbon Project went beyond our wildest expectations. Its stated objectives were encapsulated in 3 As: awareness, acceptance and action. That is to say, awareness for the need for ex-offenders to be given second chances to make good; acceptance of ex-offenders back to their families and communities and action to help support the cause represented by the yellow ribbon, whether it was as simple as to wear the yellow ribbon, to provide employments for ex-offenders or to volunteer one's service to help inmates and ex-offenders. Public surveys done over the years had proven that the Yellow Ribbon Project had raised public awareness on re-integrative issues, promoted acceptance of ex-offenders back into their families, communities and the work-force and garnered public action to assist ex-offenders.

The success of the Yellow Ribbon Project did not escape the attention of prison colleagues from overseas. We received many enquiries on how to run a similar public campaign elsewhere. In 2007, the year I retired from the Prison Service, we published the Yellow Ribbon Project manual to serve as a how-to guide to overseas colleagues as well as the next generation of Prison Officers. It was an opportunity for us to identify the critical success factors of the project. Some of the key ones are: a passionate core team; the involvement of inmates and ex-inmates; the simple and consistent messaging through an iconic symbol of a yellow ribbon; the skilful use of the media; the participation of celebrities, political leaders and the President; and community partnership.

One important lesson I learnt through the Yellow Ribbon Project was, to engender action, reason alone is insufficient. One must touch the emotions to make a real difference. The powerful personal testimonies of those who had undertaken the difficult journeys of being released from prison proved effective in touching emotions. The awards events where family members were invited to prison to be part of the awards ceremony usually left no dry eyes in the house. Through the Yellow Ribbon Project, we succeeded in promoting a cause that transcended organisational boundaries and individual interests. It fulfilled the objectives (the 3As) identified when we first started: creating awareness, acceptance and engendering action to help ex-offenders.

CHAPTER THIRTEEN

SOME INSIGHTS INTO REHABILITATION

Many people are fascinated by the notion of rehabilitation. At the core of the matter is the question: how can people be changed? The belief that people cannot change is encapsulated by that immortal saying: "a leopard cannot change its spots!" To change people in normal everyday life is indeed difficult, if not impossible. Life has too many temptations and distractions and most people are not able to pursue a course of change single-mindedly. Prison, however, provides a unique environment in which change is not only possible, but an everyday occurrence. At one fell stroke, a prisoner is stripped of his or her past and given a fresh opportunity to restart. You cannot have a more egalitarian society than the one in prison, where education, social standing, wealth, affiliations and profession do not matter one bit. Everyone is treated as equals and nobody gets better treatment because of who they were before they come to prison.

Rehabilitation would be impossible in many prisons in the world where control is in the hands of the dominating gang, or worse a terrorist organisation, rather than the prison authority. To run rehabilitation successfully, a safe and motivating prison environment is a prerequisite. If a prisoner has to be subservient to gangland bosses, fears for his safety, and has to try to placate his gang members all the time, he would be better off keeping his criminal mindset even when he is in prison. That is why during my tenure, I instituted the zero tolerance policy against gang affiliation in the Singapore prisons. A prisoner had to go through the ritual of declaring and renouncing his gang affiliation while under incarceration. Those who refused to renounce their gang affiliation would be isolated from the main body of prisoners and stuck at the lowest level of privileges under the Progressive Privileges System. When I implemented this policy, many among my staff thought that I was trying to placate the old "security" camp. In truth, I was totally focused on making rehabilitation doable.

The Progressive Privileges System was another important initiative I implemented during my tenure. I came across the idea when I first visited prisons in the UK and Canada in 1999. I realised the disciplinary system then in Singapore was over-reliant on punishments to deter breaches of discipline. We needed a system of positive reinforcement of good behaviour to counter-balance the punishment regime. The details of the system are complicated but the principle is simple. All privileges, like the frequencies of letter writing, number of visitors, number of hours of television watching, entitlement of canteen items, and books and library visits, can be tweaked according to how well a prisoner behaves and for how long. Prison is such a highly regulated environment that no aspect of daily life is outside the control of the prison authority. The possible combinations and permutations of according privileges to well-behaved prisoners were immense.

When a prisoner worked his way up to the highest level of privileges, where he got to meet visitors face-to-face rather than through a video camera or a glass panel and where he could engage in work, education and recreation all his waking hours rather than being confined in a cell, the loss of privileges could be very painful. Such positive reinforcement of good behaviour is also more in tandem with a rehabilitative approach. Interestingly, the most elaborate system of progressive privileges I had seen was in China. There, every little achievement on the part of prison inmates was scored in numerical form and the scores were posted on a large board in a common area. No prisoner needed to guess how he fared compared to the others. I thought that was real transparency. These two important prisoner management tools, namely the zero tolerance policy against gang affiliation and the Progressive Privileges System made for a more secure prison environment which is an essential backdrop to rehabilitation.

Let us go back to the question: "How can a person be changed?" As usual, if you break down a problem into its component parts and deal with each part in turn, the problem does not appear to be so daunting any more. At the core of offending is addiction. By far the most prevalent addiction problem among prisoners is drug addiction. There are other kinds of addictions which are prevalent but are less well understood. For example, addiction to gambling, addiction to sexual perversion and addiction to easy money and fast women (or men as the case may be) commonly known as the criminal lifestyle just to name a few. Rehabilitation programmes would first have to deal with these addiction problems. The way to overcome an addiction problem is to educate the addicts on the mechanics of their addiction and its consequences, to open their eyes to how victims and loved ones are hurt by their actions and behaviours. Once they accept that they have an addiction problem and are aware of its pitfalls, they will then be in a position to set life goals and craft an action plan to rid themselves of their addiction. This approach is known to psychologists as the cognitive behavioural approach. Since I am not a psychologist, I will stick to a layman's exposition of my personal experience.

Key to the message of change is how loved ones are hurt by the prisoner's under-contribution or non-contribution to their roles in life. The two essential elements here are loved ones and life roles. If the prisoner has neither, then the chances of rehabilitation are slim indeed. Fortunately, the absolute majority of prisoners do have these elements somewhere or some time in their lives and they can be given the opportunity to rediscover them.

When I attended an International Corrections and Prisons Association (ICPA) conference in Edinburgh in 2005, I attended a talk by Dr Tony Watt on his "Good Lives Model". I thought I had finally found the intellectual anchor to rehabilitation. His idea was simple; a prisoner's desire to fulfil his life roles will drive his rehabilitation efforts. In other words, the desire to become a better father, a better son or a better husband will keep a person on the road of recovery. His thesis squared with our own research findings that the determination to change often comes as a result of a life changing event, for example, the death of a loved one, a son failing in his studies, a wife seeking a divorce etc. Sometimes, that life changing event is accompanied by

Chapter Thirteen

a religious conversion. Together, they become a powerful force for change. The Singapore Prison Service has since been working closely with Dr Tony Watt to introduce more of his ideas into its rehabilitation programmes.

If family and loved ones are such an important component to rehabilitation, it makes sense for the prison authority to help prisoners maintain family ties and facilitate interactions between prisoners and their loved ones. One key initiative here was the introduction of tele-visits. The idea was quite simple. Up till then, family members who wanted to visit their loved ones in prison must come to the prisons where they were incarcerated. This could be quite difficult for some as they had to make the effort to come, often having to take leave on a working day. The elderly and disabled found it particularly difficult to walk the long distance into the prison compound. Tele-visits simply use video-conferencing to connect the inmates in prison and the visitors at locations that were more accessible and convenient. This encouraged more visits and thus enhanced family ties. In fact, we planned to roll out home tele-visit after the initial success of tele-visits based on dedicated facilities because by then, broad-band internet had made the quality of image on an ordinary home computer acceptable. This was however stopped by the Ministry. Unsurprisingly, the Ministry was worried about the loss of control when visitors could tele-visit from their home. It would not be possible to control who would be there and whether the conversation was recorded without authorisation.

During my tenure, I also introduced open visits where prisoners at the highest levels in the Progressive Privileges System could meet their family members face to face. On fathers' day and mothers' day, children were allowed to come into the prisons and celebrate the occasion with their parents. These were on top of the awards events under the Yellow Ribbon Project that I already mentioned. In fact, my desire was that every excuse should be found to strengthen family ties and help prisoners realise what their life roles were.

Towards the end of my tenure, we started family service centres at various prisons to help prisoners' family with their problems. These centres provided family counselling and operate assistance schemes to help families cope with hardship. They were outsourced to various Volunteer Welfare Organisations who had experience operating similar centres in the community. Initially, very few family members of prisoners would approach the centres on their own accord. The operators had to take the initiative to reach out to waiting family members who came to visit their loved ones. I expected this situation to improve when people became more familiar with the help that they could get from these centres.

An even earlier initiative was the Play and Wait Programme (PAW) as a result of collaboration with a volunteer welfare organisation *Save the Children Singapore*. Young children who accompanied their relatives to visit their parents often had to wait for their turn to visit. Instead of wasting that time, they were offered a play room where social workers would take the opportunity of playing with them to provide listening ears and counselling on their emotional problems because of their absent parents. This programme was eventually adopted by the Salvation Army and they are still at it today. These were all done to give prisoners a chance to renew and restart after they were released from prisons.

CHAPTER THIRTEEN

What about those prisoners who have no family and loved ones? As I mentioned, they can be helped to re-discover them. Sometimes, a surrogate familial structure can replace what had been lost. No one begins life without family and loved ones. The possibility for new familial associations always exists. I would say that during my tenure, this aspect was still work in progress. However, one obvious way to reconstruct familial ties was through religion where new loved ones in the family of God or gods could be found. During my tenure, I worked with all the major mainstream religions to enhance the spiritual aspect of prisoners' lives. One could be on dangerous ground here unless one is sensitive and even-handed in dealing with different religious groups. However, the risks were worth it as they sometimes reaped handsome rewards. For example, we had heard that some Latin American countries had experimented with faith-based programmes and found them effective. After studying the matter, we too decided to experiment with faith-based programmes. We offered all the mainstream religious organisations an opportunity to learn about such programmes and structured their own. It involved having religious teachers working within the prison on a full-time basis for a period of up to six months and immersed those who took part deeply in their religious teaching. By all accounts, these programmes had been very successful in bringing about change in those who took part.

After taking care of the emotional and spiritual aspects of a prisoner's rehabilitation, we must now focus on things more mundane, like education and skills training. These are ways to help prisoners fulfil their desire to play their life roles better. It could be done through the Prison School, the education and training programmes in all prisons and the prison industry. One of the more successful programmes run by SCORE was the Train and Place Programme. Employers came to the prisons, selected potential employees before they were released and trained them while they were still serving sentence. When they were released, they could immediately step into their jobs. A good example was the training of landscape technicians. Within the fence of a prison cluster and in between the prison blocks, there was ample green space for these technicians to undergo training. The gifted ones could earn a very decent wage when they were released from prison. Another very successful vocation was as food handlers in the food industry. Food is recession-proof and in food-loving Singapore, it is an evergreen vocation. SCORE dedicated itself to finding and developing more of such vocations in vocational training and in the prison industry so that released prisoners would be able to be weaned off their past criminal lifestyle and earn their own wages.

Programmes in prison are only half the story in the quest for rehabilitation. Once a prisoner is released, real life is no bed of roses. Aftercare is as important as in-care. I had mentioned the Case Management Framework and the Yellow Ribbon Project earlier. The Yellow Ribbon Fund and the ex-prisoners' co-operative, the Industrial and Services Co-operative (ISCOS) helped prisoners and their families find financial help and business opportunities and were essential elements in the aftercare arena. A company known as RE Holdings was established by ISCOS with a few other shareholders to invest in companies that would employ released prisoners if they had difficulty finding a job. The R in RE Holdings stands for Re-enter and the E Enterprise. The idea of a Re-enterprise resonated with an audience of correctional professionals when I presented it at a conference in Baltimore in 2006. In my view, these aftercare efforts were still work in progress and much more could be done. In recent years, after stabilising the in-care system, the Singapore Prison Service turned its attention more to the aftercare system. I am sure we will hear more of this in the years to come under the new administration.

When I first came to the Prison Service, I believed that rehabilitation was the only hope to stop the revolving door. However, I did not hold out much hope that most prisoners could be rehabilitated. Like many Police Officers, I believed that it was impossible to change hardcore criminals and I thought at least 30% of the prisoners were hardcore. Looking back, I now believe that 95% of prisoners serving sentence at any one time can be changed. The only question is whether we are determined enough to do so. The other important perspective is, when we talk about changing people, we usually think of it as changing them to something that will fit a mental mould that we have constructed. In other words, we want them to change in our way. Dr Tony Watt clearly showed that the best way was to allow them to change in their own ways as long as the ultimate objective of becoming responsible citizens was met.

CHAPTER FOURTEEN

END OF TENURE

In early 2007, the permanent secretary of the Ministry of Home Affairs, Benny Lim, spoke to me over lunch. He offered me a secondment to a government-linked private sector company — Aetos Security Management Pte Ltd ("Aetos"). If I accepted the offer, I would leave the Prison Service six months before my retirement to give way to Ng Joo Hee. Just before this conversation, my relationship with the Ministry had become quite testy. It seemed to me that this was an indication that the Ministry had enough of me and I must confess that at the point in time, the feeling was mutual. I accepted the offer. In return, I was given the opportunity to attend the Advance Management Programme in INSEAD, Fontainebleau (near Paris) to prepare me for my foray into the private sector. I left the Prison Service in November 2007 to take up the post of CEO and Executive Director in Aetos; however, I only retired from the Civil Service in May 2008. Just before my departure, my deputy and close associate Jason Wong accepted an offer from the Ministry of Community Development, Youth and Sports (MCYS) to be seconded there for three years. He subsequently requested for his service to be transferred permanently from the Prison Service to MCYS. He would later accept an offer to transfer his service to MCYS, never to return to the Prison Service.

The Prison Service I left behind was very different from the one I inherited. By 2008, the Prison Service had garnered numerous organisational excellence awards, including the Singapore Quality Award (SQA). The award that gave me the most satisfaction, however, came from Hewitt Associates' Best Employers study in Singapore. The Prison Service was found to be one of the top 10 employers in Singapore through a survey of its own employees randomly sampled by the organiser. The Prison Service scored high in employee engagement and was ranked alongside companies famous for their service standards and culture of excellence such as the Four Seasons Hotel, the Ritz Carlton Hotel and Raffles Hotel. Unlike the award process in SQA in which the assessment process could be stage managed to a great extent, the Hewitt survey was more objective and not easily given to manipulation. In fact, we took part in the survey more as a benchmarking exercise than as an attempt to win an award. The Prison Service's win attracted some media attention at the time as it was the first and only public organisation to receive the award. I suppose, loosely speaking, the Prison Service may be considered a hotel group of sorts.

By the time I left, the inmate population in the prison system had dropped from more than 17000 to about 13000. Most tellingly, the last measured 2-year recidivism rate had dropped to 24.9% compared to the 44.1% when I first arrived. The most remarkable improvement in recidivism rate was in the treatment of drug addiction — where once it was more than 50%, the rate had dropped to a low of 20%. A fully functional rehabilitation system had been built and was showing results.

In terms of infrastructure, the manpower saving design and advance technology deployed in the new Changi Prison Complex could serve as a template for large scale prison developments anywhere. In operationalising Cluster A of the complex, I decided that the team that would eventually manage the cluster should also work out the plans on how to operate the cluster. This is different from the usual approach of having a separate planning team and handing the plan over to a frontline team to operationalise. I had seen enough examples of the pitfalls of the traditional approach where every problem in practice would be blamed on the plan or the planning team. The new approach proved to be the correct one.

The organisation also had a working corporate planning process that generated many ground breaking strategies in prison management and rehabilitation. By then, the original 3-year plan had been reviewed twice. A summary of the strategic framework over my tenure in the Prison Service is in Annex 14.1. This framework was also used to develop the balanced scorecard that the Prison Service used to measure its performance.

The so-called 3I (ideas, improvements and innovations) process was pouring out initiatives on how to implement and supplement those strategies. A full-fledged Psychological Branch comprising 20 psychologists headed by Timothy Leo had been established to spearhead research and programme development. The research team, ably led by Dr Neo Lee Hong had published a number of insightful papers and developed new tools to assess inmates. Our success was well articulated in international forums and the

MAKING OF CAPTAINS OF LIVES

Singapore Prison system had been widely accepted by our colleagues internationally as world class and one of the most cost effective. Our active involvement in the International Corrections and Prisons Association (ICPA) and the Asia and Pacific Conference of Correctional Administrators (APCCA) helped to garner the recognition that the Singapore system provided a benchmark against which prison systems of the world could be measured.

The most important achievement of all was not systemic or infrastructural, but cultural. As shown in the Hewitt survey, Prison Officers were among the most engaged employees in Singapore. The cultural change was all the more startling when one compared the present situation, like I did, with the situation nine years ago. No, the "security" camp had not quite been completely vanquished, but the critical mass of Prison Officers believed in rehabilitation and they put that belief into action. This transformation could be illustrated by the story of Desmond Chin, a capable young officer at the time who was to play an important role in the whole endeavour later. Desmond missed most of the early action because he was seconded to the Ministry of Home Affairs when I arrived on the scene. He only returned to the Prison Service in October 1999. He suddenly discovered that the Prison Service had changed during his years away. In the first breakfast meeting attended by him, he remonstrated with me not to eat the food before us because "it was prepared by prisoners". Little did he realise that the us-versus-them mindset had been my pet grouse at the time. Needless to say, he was roundly reprimanded by me for being impertinent.

Desmond became my operations chief in August 2001 and in October 2005, he became the CEO of SCORE, taking over that portfolio from Jason Wong. He was picked for the job because it was my assessment that he had been converted to the cause of rehabilitation and could be entrusted with running the prison industry and the vocational training programmes so crucial in the rehabilitation of offenders. He was still in that job when I left the Prison Service. He had become a champion of rehabilitation, producing food handlers for the food industry, landscape technicians for the landscaping industry and many more. He was completely transformed and totally different from that officer who refused to eat the food prepared by prisoners five years ago.

This change in culture also helped make Prison Service a choice employer. Many young men and women who joined the Prison Service were motivated by the idea that they would become the captains of lives and they would help prisoners escape a subsequent sentence in prison. The enlargement of Prison Service's talent pool would stand the Service in good stead for years to come. The general improvement in the quality of prison officers and the more open culture also lead to many grassroots initiatives in support of the rehabilitation course. For example, frontline officers started a new programme called "Beautiful Minds" in the Changi Prison Complex. This programme targeted inmates who were psychotic, for rehabilitation by art therapy. Many of the art works in the Yellow Ribbon Art Exhibition were the work of these inmates. I once visited these inmates and I was struck by how normal and motivated they were. Another example of grassroots initiative was the Centre of Performing Art set up in the Changi Prison Complex. Being a music lover myself, I was particularly pleased about the formation of the choir as part of this initiative. Today, this centre continues to produce the talents who perform in the various Yellow Ribbon and other public events.

Near the end of my tenure, the new leadership model was ready to be implemented. It had taken us two years of working with two teams of consultants to finally produce a leadership model that would guide the men and women in leadership positions to be better leaders. The model captured all that a good leader should be most succinctly and I believe it has wider application than the Prison Service. When I took over as Director, I was not satisfied with the appraisal system that we inherited. One of the objectives of developing the new leadership model was to improve the appraisal of staff particularly those in the upper echelon. The project began with the mapping of the core competencies that Prison Officers must have through interviews with the best officers in the service. The core competencies were then grouped and classified before being consolidated into a single diagram in the shape of a sail boat. I shall have more to say about the leadership model in the next chapter.

Another unfinished business at the end of my tenure was the development of a re-integrative potential index. I always had doubts about measuring the success of rehabilitation by using a lag indicator like the recidivism rate. By the time the recidivism rate of a cohort is known, the cohort would have already been released for two years. How does such an indicator help us to fine-tune our rehabilitation efforts? The other problem with recidivism rate is that it is dependent on the quality of the cohort. When the easier cases have been successfully rehabilitated, the more difficult cases will be left behind. You should then expect to have higher recidivism rates over time. So clearly, going forward, whether the recidivism rate is higher or lower does not tell us very much about the success of rehabilitation. I thought it was possible to construct a tool to measure the change in the re-integrative potential of inmate. This would provide a lead indicator predictive of success and help us fine-tune our efforts. A lot of work had gone into developing and constructing this tool and it was being field tested when I left.

Annex 14.1: Strategic Framework for Action

Period	FY 2000 — FY2002	FY2003 — FY2005	FY2006 —
Focal Areas	a. Enhanced Operational Capabilities b. Staff Development Structure c. Integrated Incare d. Coordinated Aftercare	a. Enhancing Inmate Management Capability b. Maximising Inmates' Reintegration Potential c. Developing Staff to Make a Difference d. Preventing Offending and RE-offending	
Key Levers	a. Technology b. Knowledge Management c. Community Resources	a. Mass Media b. Knowledge Management c. Community Resources d. Technology	

(Continued)

Annex 14.1 (Continued)

Period	FY 2000 — FY2002	FY2003 — FY2005	FY2006 —
Anchor Projects	a. Housing Unit Management System	a. Coping with Increased Overcrowding	a. Developing Housing Units as Transformational Environment
	b. Classification System	b. Seamless Throughcare System	b. Building a Nimble & Flexible Organisation
	c. 24-hour Operations Centre at HQ	c. Integrating Inmates as part of our Human Resources	c. Winning the Hearts & Minds of the Community
	d. Female Deployment	d. Capabilities in Managing Alternative Sentencing Options	
	e. Ethics Structure	e. Increasing Employability of Inmates	
	f. Outsourcing of non-core functions	f. Engaging Inmates' Families	
	g. ZTP (Zero Tolerance Policy) against gangs		
	h. Tail-end Home Detention		
	i. Prison Management System (PMS)		

CHAPTER FIFTEEN

THE LEADERSHIP MODEL

The leadership model was such an important issue that I think it warrants a separate chapter. When I became the head of Singapore Prison Service, I thought that it was important to determine what effective leaders were like in the Prison Service so that their skills could be documented and transferred to those who came after them. The leadership model could also form the basis of the appraisal of the top talents in the Prison Service and identify their development needs. In the earlier years when I was busy trying to determine the broad approach to reform the prison system, I had no time to focus on this matter. By the time I came round to it, it was near the end of my tenure. The study I mentioned in the last chapter did produce something very worthwhile and not entirely expected. Unfortunately, I would soon leave the Prison Service and had no time left to see through its implementation.

The leadership model boat was christened "MV Sublime". Each of the letters represents an essential leadership quality. MV representing mission and vision, made up the sail of the leadership boat. The hull was made up of the letters SUBLIME. S stands for shape the future. U stands for unleash potential. B stands for build bridges. L is leverage capability. I is inculcate nimbleness. M is master self and E is endeavour to succeed. In addition, four essential items in the boat represent traits that a leader must have. The rope represents attitude to serve, the binding force of us all. The rudder represents the courage to steer in the right direction. The life buoy represents like ability that will bring others on board and the anchor represents integrity that keeps us steady. I will describe each of these qualities in turn in the following paragraphs.

(MV) A good leader must walk the talk of the mission and vision. That is fairly self evident. However, many colleagues I spoke to in INSEAD did not understand the difference between mission and vision. Many companies had mission statements and many felt that vision and mission are interchangeable in meaning. Having gone through the visioning exercise, I was quite clear about the usefulness of having two separate and distinct mission and vision statements. The mission statement should articulate the values the organisation is currently adding to their clients and society. The vision statement should paint the picture of what the organisation aspires to be in the long term. I had use the matrix of vision elements against mission elements as a planning tool. There is no doubt in my mind that both statements are critical and need to be co-created and co-determined by the key stakeholders of the organisation.

(S) A person gains the right to be a leader because he sees further into the future. He does not leave the future to the wind and the wave, but actively steer a course in the here and now towards the vision. I see this quality as the most important quality in the top leader. (U) A leader must be a nurturer, who sees it as his job to make sure that everyone of his followers has the space to develop their talent and achieve their potential. He must do so out of a genuine love and concern for his followers and in the interest of the organisation. (B) A leader must be able to build bridges across groups and between individuals so that different groups and people with very different interests can be aligned to achieve a common objective and operate in the same team. (L) A leader must be able to use the strength of a follower to the fullest while avoid giving him tasks that require him to operate in his areas of weakness. For example, if an officer does not speak well in public but is able to be persuasive to a small group, he should not be sent to make public speeches but given small groups to steer. (I) A leader must be nimble, able to deal with ambiguity and make decisions with inadequate information. He needs to hone his instincts so that he is able to rely on his judgement as much as the data his has at hand. He must be able to see the broad picture without neglecting the important details. He must have an open mind, able to digest divergent views and come to a convergent decision. The ability to be nimble is something that needs to be inculcated deliberately over time and in order to retain this nimbleness, a leader must be able to preach to himself about maintaining an open mind and look for inflection points that will require him to change course.

(M) Mastering self is about life-long learning. A leader must never be complacent but constantly endeavour to master all the skills and knowledge necessary for him to do his job better. For example, most officers in uniform are good at managing operations but very few are comfortable with financial matters and dealing with the balance sheets. I had the same problem when I had to be responsible for the Prison Service budget as its head. I had to force myself to go for courses and read up and digest all the theories of good financial management and understand all the budget numbers. In time, I became completely comfortable with financial matters. A more subtle form of mastery is overcoming one's natural inclination in order to do the job better. I was one of those who had been shy from childhood and was not comfortable making small talks in social gatherings. In the prison reform journey, it became absolutely necessary for me to win friends and influence people. I had to master my natural shyness and learn to be comfortable with people in all kinds of social settings. (E) The will to succeed is the critical attribute in any leader. It describes an attitude that never gives up and a willingness to run any gauntlet in order to lead the followers to the promised land. Endeavour to succeed also speaks of boldness to try, moral courage to act decisively and the tenacity to stay the course despite adversities. I think the qualities represented by MV SUBLIME are fairly easy to accept and many good appraisal systems would have some elements of these qualities.

Among the four on-board items in MV SUBLIME, integrity and courage are also well understood. Integrity is about doing the right things with the right motive in the interest of the collective good. Courage is about taking half chances when success is not assured. One of my most used phrases to describe courage is "faith energises, fear paralyses". Courage comes from the firm belief that the cause is the right one and what one is going to do is needful for the cause. The two attributes that are less obvious are attitude to serve and likeability. Attitude to serve is not quite the same as servant leadership, a term that has been much abused and misunderstood. When I interacted with trainees who were about to become senior officers, I often asked them why they wanted to become leaders. The most common answer I received was that they wanted to be in a position to make things happen, exercise power or make more contribution. The answers showed that the officers were quite obviously focused on what they as leaders could achieve. The attitude to serve answers this question differently. It is focused on what leadership can achieve for the followers and what leaders and followers can achieve together as a team. Such an externally centred attitude is what makes the difference between an ordinary leader and a really good leader. Likeability comes to fore when the team comes face to face with a serious challenge, when success is not assured and when risks have to be taken. People will continue to give their support and risk their own career and reputation for the leader only when they truly like the leader. When the chips are down, only affective bonds will have the followers and supporters coalesce around the leader.

Each of the quality I wrote of can be identified and developed to a certain extent. Not knowing about them is sure to limit a leader's chance of success. My own personal take on leadership in the Prison Service was contained in a speech I gave in an international conference. When I gave that speech, I was two weeks from stepping down from my office and it was a time for reflection. I attach this speech titled "Leadership & Innovation" in Annex 15.1 as an illustration of my thinking on the leadership model.

Annex 15.1: Leadership & Innovation* (an edited excerpt)

Introduction

I have spent nine years at the helm of the Singapore Prison Service. These nine years had been very eventful ones as I led the service in the profound change of embracing rehabilitation of ex-offenders as our core function. One of the issues constantly on my radar scope during the change process was leadership. Is there something that makes a good correctional leader unique or is a good leader a good leader in any field?

Overview of Presentation

My conclusion after all these years is that all good leaders share common characteristics, regardless of the fields they are in. However, for good correctional leaders, four pivotal elements amongst all the other common leadership characteristics stand out. They are:

> Character,
> Alliance-Building,
> Innovation, and
> Thought Leadership.

At the Heart of Leadership — Character

If I say that character is at the heart of leadership, I believe few of you would disagree. Warren Bennis said that "successful leadership is not about being tough or soft, sensitive or

---

*Speech at ICPA (International Corrections and Prisons Association), October 2007, Bangkok.

assertive, but about a set of attributes. First and foremost is character." These words are even truer of leaders in helping professions. Having a good character is as much about possessing good intrinsic qualities as it is about constantly bettering oneself. We often find successful organisations having leaders with a good heart. Whether an organisation has an altruistic mission is sometimes secondary. What is important is their core ideology, and how their ideology contributes to the betterment of mankind.

Charles Handy once said that "the companies that survive longest are the ones that work out what they uniquely can give to the world — not just growth or money but their excellence, their respect for others, or their ability to make people happy. Some call those things a soul." Walt Disney is one such organisation. Merck, the pharmaceutical giant, is another one founded on the core ideology that the medicine is for the people, and not for profits. Their founders have left strong legacies behind, not just for their future generations of staff, but for mankind.

Integrity — Our Anchor

For corrections, we have progressed from providing custodial care to embracing rehabilitation as an equally important goal. In order for officers to perform these dual roles effectively, leaders need to operate with guiding principles well-grounded in morality. Abraham Lincoln said that "nearly all men can stand adversity, but if you want to test a man's character, give him power." Correctional leaders have strong power and authority inherent in their roles. They are in a position to grant favour and exact gratification for themselves. However, I am sure all of us in this room agree that there is no room for unethical behaviours of any kind in a good correctional service, let alone corruption. How do we know that something we do is unethical? There is always the much cited "sleep" test. If it keeps you awake at night, it is probably unethical. I will venture an even more useful test: if you do not want your behaviour to be on headline news, it is probably unethical.

Moral Courage — The Rudder that Guides Us

In the Singapore Prison Service, we set up an Ethics Structure in 2000 to provide guidelines to officers in their daily interactions with inmates, inmates' families and fellow colleagues. In this structure, there are various channels for officers to disclose breaches in ethics, including a direct bypass channel for officers to disclose any observed impropriety to the Deputy Director of Prisons. It requires moral courage to expose yourself or another officer in this way.

Moral courage can also be demonstrated when nothing seems wrong. Many of you will be familiar with our Yellow Ribbon Project. We did not conceive the project because something was a miss. We did it because this was in line with our vision, because this will help ex-offenders and create positive ripple effects in society. At that time, it was a radical idea. The public was still sceptical about ex-offenders' propensity to change. Nevertheless, I saw the faith and moral courage of the then CEO of our partner agency, SCORE, Mr Jason Wong, as he championed the project. Though I gave my full support to Jason, many others were apprehensive. Together with Jason, my team took that leap of faith into uncharted territory. Today, many ex-offenders are benefitting from the project. More are offered jobs and given opportunities to display their talents.

CHAPTER FIFTEEN

Attitude to Serve — The Correctional Leader's Calling

I believe the purpose of a leader is to better the lives of his followers. Leaders should always ask what would deliver happiness to his followers and lead them to it. As correctional leaders, we serve our followers, the community, and a social cause. When I first took over the helm as the Director of Prisons in November 1998, the first question I asked was, "what future do people in the Singapore Prison Service want for the organisation?" I saw an immediate need to bring people together to dialogue. That was the visioning exercise involving more than 700 staff, which saw the birth of our vision. I was only a facilitator in the process, as the vision was forged by the staff. With this vision, my job as Director was to lead them on this exciting journey towards the common destination. Once we set our minds on our vision, getting there is non-negotiable. Though some might become faint-hearted before reaching the destination, we need to place the larger cause above our self-interests.

Likeability — Importance of Good Relationships

Having an upright moral character with a strong attitude to serve is sometimes not enough. Unless a leader has that elusive quality called charisma, they need to be likeable to be effective. When I say "likeable", it is not the same as "popular". Likeability is the ability to work effectively with people from diverse backgrounds, maintain a pleasant demeanour and demonstrate respect for others in all their interactions. It is also about how to behave appropriately in different situations. Correctional leaders need to influence not just inmates and staff, but also win the community at large towards the correctional cause. We will fail in our mission if we are not likeable.

Mastering Self

To cultivate good character, leaders need to be self-aware and seek constant improvements to become a wiser person. Gene Mauch, an American baseball player, has said that "you can't lead anyone else farther than you have gone yourself". A wise leader who commits to self-improvement can lead better. I always believe we should spend more time to develop our strengths rather than to fix our weaknesses. However, the road to wisdom requires us to constantly improve ourselves. While we will never be perfect, we can always try.

As part of my journey towards "self-mastery", I challenge myself daily to do things against my natural inclination. As a person, I am naturally shy and uncomfortable with social interactions. However, a leader needs to put his duty above comfort. Understanding that networking is key to building alliances and support for our cause, I made it a point to attend conferences and public events to find opportunities to further our goals. Within my organisation, I meet management and ground officers regularly through weekly meetings and monthly institutional visits. These interactions are important, though not pleasurable to me.

Building Bridges

Corrections of today can no longer operate in silos. We have had to answer questions about the rationale of our processes and the effectiveness of our programmes. For instance, with the increased number of youth offenders in recent years, we received more queries on our youth treatment programmes from many quarters. One of our Superintendents was even summoned to court to explain the treatment regime for our reformative trainees. I believe many correction systems in the world are also facing increasing levels of public scepticism and scrutiny. Thus, the challenge for today's and future correctional leaders lies in their ability to build strong alliances to win the hearts and minds of the community towards the correctional cause. Winning the mind is a relatively easy task, compared to winning the heart.

Alliance-Building with Key Stakeholders

To quote a personal experience, the visioning exercise we had in 1999 was anything but smooth-sailing. We faced much difficulty in convincing a few key stakeholders to buy in to our vision. Some were afraid that prisons would go "soft". However, I knew that what we wanted was the right thing to do and we stayed our course. The next thing we did was to build alliances with people and organisations more sympathetic to our cause. One by one, we won their support until we finally found enough allies to advocate for us. Looking back, things would not have moved at that time if not for these allies who shared our beliefs. We need external advocates for our cause. They are more credible and more likely to be listened to by the public than any official figure.

Alliance-building is an ongoing process. Getting support from our key partners is good but not enough. We need to involve them at a deeper level. Prisons can only provide rehabilitation care for as long as the inmates are in prison. Once they are out, the community is where their lives are lived. Recognising the importance to enrol our partners fully in our vision, I initiated two retreats involving six agencies and NGOs (Non-government Organisation) in 2000. At the retreats, we engaged in dialogues to examine how collectively, we could achieve better coordination between in-care and aftercare. The retreats resulted in the formation of the network for Community Action for the Rehabilitation of Ex-offenders, or CARE network for short. Members of this network were mainly the Chairmen, Directors and CEOs of the relevant key agencies. We held regular discussions as we aligned our work towards our common vision. The formation of the CARE network was a major milestone for us. It had brought about greater synergy and allowed closer coordination of the work amongst the agencies.

Sharing Knowledge and Best Practices

Besides building strong alliances with key partners, we also build bridges to share knowledge. There is much to learn from others in our industry, such as having this conference to network, share knowledge and best practices. There is much more to learn outside our industry, as new and different perspectives will always add richness to our thinking and possibly shift our mental paradigms. By hearing fresh perspectives from others, we run lesser risk of being "boxed in" by our accustomed *modus operandi* and avoid the pitfall of corporate blindness in the long run. Working in prisons does tend to box us in.

Leadership Series in Singapore Prison Service

For that reason, we started a Leadership Series this year. On this platform, eminent corporate leaders are invited to speak on their leadership experiences. We had the privilege of listening to the CEO of Alexandra Hospital and the Chairman of one of the Top 50 Enterprising Companies in Singapore. They shared their thoughts and stories on leadership and we learned a lot from them. One thing that Mr Liak of Alexandra Hospital shared was "don't take yourself too seriously". What he meant was, our actions should never be motivated by hurt pride. Indeed, while it is important to take work seriously, we should live and experience the fun and spontaneity of life where possible.

Innovation as a Key to Avoid Success Traps

In order to avoid becoming stagnated by success, it is important to ensure newness in thoughts. This will translate into innovation at work. To build a progressive culture that supports innovation, a sense of discomfort and discontentment with status quo needs to be engendered. We also need to reward people for innovative ideas and allow some failures as they experiment with innovation. Allow me to share two examples to illustrate the point.

Example 1: The Story of the Prison School

As some of you would know, we built a Prison School in 2000 founded on the concept of "school first, prison second". This concept was unorthodox in the correctional field at the time as most prison officers believed that inmates' education should operate within the operating model of a prison. My belief was — there needs to be a centralisation of teaching resources to create a conducive learning environment. I set up a taskforce to institute new systems and processes for the Prison School modelled after an independent school. Today, I am glad that the school has become a model of success.

Example 2: Ideas, Improvements and Innovations

A few months after taking over my job, I made it compulsory for each institution and staff unit to take turns to present innovative ideas at our weekly Breakfast Meetings. This created that sense of discomfort among my staff, which was necessary for progress. The ideas would then be evaluated based on their innovativeness, practicality and relevance to the organisation's goals. Only the better ideas would pass the assessment and the unit that failed to get their ideas through would have to present again at the next meeting. Through this platform, many ideas benefitting the organisations had since been implemented. One example is the introduction of "News Behind Bars", which is a monthly video newsletter for the inmates. This is now used as an internal communication channel to inmates where events such as the Song Writing Competitions are publicised. Interviews with celebrities and people who can act as role models are also featured. Another example was the broadcasting of "intel alerts" to inmates to see if they can help the Police track down suspects or give clues to unsolved cases. The idea of creating a Specialised Treatment Environment for young offenders was also mooted through this platform.

The Transitory Nature of Innovation

Innovation has a shelf life. We need to constantly re-invent ourselves and progress from good to better. We must be prepared to replace proven practices with new ones. This is sometimes called "creative destruction". We must be ready for change at all time as the future will always bring something new that has to be met with new thinking and new ideas. This brings me to my final point on "thought" leadership.

Thought Leadership

As John Quincy put it "if your actions or thoughts inspire others to dream more, learn more, do more and become more, you are a leader." This sums up the essence of thought leadership. Today, leaders will no longer be respected just for being in authority. We can expect the next generation to challenge our ways of doing things and our operating models. It is not enough just to be good at what we do. Leaders must be able to articulate philosophies and ideologies can change organisations, people's lives or even the world. Thought leaders have an influence that extends beyond the execution of instructions. They shape other leaders' thinking and change the course of events. To a certain extent, the Yellow Ribbon Project has shaped societal views on ex-offenders. Quite a few colleagues told me that the Yellow Ribbon Project could not happen in their countries because of the different political culture. Maybe these colleagues should try to exercise thought leadership and see what comes out of it.

The Paradox of Success

I have talked about the key ingredients that make up a good leader who will lead his organisation to success. However, success is not the destination. In fact, success poses a grave danger to organisations unless we are watchful for the success traps. The Bible speaks of Moses leading his people to the promised land. It also narrated the new problems these people encountered when they reached the promised land. We must fight the human nature of becoming complacent and conceited with success. Otherwise, we are doomed to failure after the initial success. This is the timeless lesson that we must learn from history.

Creating a Nimble and Flexible Culture

I want to end this lecture by emphasising the importance of investing time on developing our people. We need to encourage people to constantly innovate to create a nimble and flexible culture that will enable us to bend to different circumstances and go around any obstacles. This is the only way we can deal with the rapid changes that lie ahead in this globalised world. This is necessary not just for corrections, but all organisations. I would like to leave you with a final quotation by Harvey Samuel Firestone, the founder of the Firestone Tire and Rubber Company — "The growth and development of people is the highest calling of leadership."

CHAPTER SIXTEEN

EPILOGUE

It has been almost four years since I left my post as Director of Prisons. The Prison Service has gone through two leadership changes in the mean time. My successor, Ng Joo Hee was in the post for two years before he was appointed the Commissioner of Police. Soh Wai Wah succeeded him as Director of Prisons in January 2010. By all accounts, the business of rehabilitation goes on. Both my successors believed in rehabilitation and had made further refinements to the system I left behind. If it were otherwise, I would be the saddest man on earth. Events seemed to suggest that all the labour and risk taking that went into reforming the prison system had not been wasted. The political leadership in the Ministry had changed too. The new administration has been much more supportive of what the Prison Service is doing and I expect greater things to come from the new leadership team.

I have since finished my stint in the private sector and stepped down as the CEO and Executive Director of Aetos Security Management Pte Ltd. It has been a most educational three and a half years and I have come to understand the ways of the private sector much better. Private sector work is certainly no public service, and I am not entirely sure if I am cut out to be a businessman. The only motivation I could find during my time with Aetos was the thought that I was helping to provide for the livelihoods of more than 2000 employees. It was fortunate that I managed to turn the company into a very profitable one during my tenure and when I left, I left behind a healthy balance sheet and a company with a bright business future.

In both the public and private sector, it has been my team that has achieved all the successes attributed to me. My individual efforts have been meagre. Most of the work was done by the people around me. To them, I am eternally grateful. Third party observers thought that I went about reforming the prison system purposefully with a blueprint in my head. In truth, there was no blueprint. It was more like building a bridge while walking on it, deciding where to go, trying out things and finding out what worked. As General Patton said, no plan survives the first shot in battle. While plans are useless, planning is essential to prepare us to face an uncertain future. At every step of the way, I had paused and taken stock and sometimes struck out in an entirely different direction from the original plan. If we insist on sticking to the original plan, how could we hope to cope with the new circumstances that would inevitably arise?

I always say that I am a remarkably lucky man. Most of the things I tried and improvised worked out well. The crucial ingredient in this kind of a game is the courage to try and the fortitude and unshakable faith that the cause is the right one even when the going gets tough. The quiet confidence emanating from that faith is what gives one's followers the courage to soldier on. I think these are the only things that I can credit myself with.

In fact, while I had played my part in changing the Singapore Prison Service, my stint there had also profoundly changed me. I become more altruistic, more appreciative of the human spirit and more inclined to service. It is fair to say that my stint in the Prison Service had inculcated the attitude to serve in me. I realised that a person is defined not so much by his personal qualities, but more by how he relates to others. I am a different person from the one who took up the post of Director of Prisons in 1999.

Looking back, I am also grateful to my then minister, Mr Wong Kan Seng who allowed me to try and reform the prison system despite his misgivings about my approach. He must have thought that I was a liberal and a zealot. In actual fact, I was neither. He could have stopped me in my track completely but he did not. Without that permission to venture forth, nothing could have been accomplished. At the time, the lack of his whole-hearted support threatened to derail my enthusiasm at several crucial junctures. Fortunately, there was Professor Ho Peng Kee who quietly championed the cause of rehabilitation in the background and provided much of the encouragement I needed. Most of all, I am grateful to all the prison officers who place their faith on me to lead them to a new future and all the volunteers and supporters of our cause for rallying around me when the going got tough.

My story also demonstrated that a civil servant who is only a mere cog in the wheel of the large machinery that is part of the national public service system can bring about profound changes if he has enough courage to try. The next chapter of my life will be written in the social service arena, where I will try to develop a system of care for the elderly and disabled as the Chairman of the board of the agency "Centre for Enabled Living". I may have stopped making a living but I have not retired. What is life without a higher cause?

ABOUT THE AUTHOR

Mr Chua Chin Kiat is currently the Chairman of the Board of Centre for Enabled Living Ltd (CEL).

Mr Chua Chin Kiat graduated with First Class Honours in the Bachelor of Science (Computer and Mathematics) from the University of Aston in 1975. He was a recipient of both the President's Scholarship and Singapore Armed Forced Overseas Scholarship. He joined the Singapore Police Force in 1977. In 1979, at the age of 26, he became the head of a police division. Mr Chua had held key appointments in the Ministry of Home Affairs Headquarters (Director of Operations) and the Singapore Police Force (Director of Manpower, Director of Operations and Director of Criminal Investigation Department). He was the Director of Prisons from 1 November 1998 to 31 October 2007 and CEO and Executive Director of Aetos Security Management from 1 November 2007 to 7 May 2011. Since stepping down from Aetos, a wholly owned subsidiary of Temasek Holdings, Mr Chua devoted his time to volunteer work, serving on the boards of CEL and Agency for Integrated Care (AIC). He was appointed the Chairman of CEL in November 2008. He was appointed Chairman of the Enabling Masterplan Steering Committee by Ministry of Community Development, Youth and Sports (MCYS) in July 2011.

Since Mr Chua took over the helm as Director of Singapore Prison Service, the Service started many new and bold initiatives which transformed the organisation into an exemplary prison system with a vision of being the "Captains of Lives". In addition, Mr Chua was a Board Member of the Singapore Corporation of Rehabilitative Enterprises (SCORE). With Mr Chua on the SCORE Board, the Prison Service and SCORE work hand in hand, combining efforts to rehabilitate inmates. Mr Chua co-chaired the Community Action for the Rehabilitation of Ex-offenders (CARE) Network with the Chairman, SCORE. The CARE network brings together the top management of helping agencies like Singapore Anti-Narcotics Association, Singapore Aftercare Association, Industrial & Services Cooperative Society and the National Council of Social Services. The Ministry of Home Affairs and the Ministry of Community, Youth and Sports are also represented in the Network.

At Aetos, Mr Chua turned the company into a profitable security services provider which provided security coverage to the Woodlands and Tuas checkpoints, the ports, Jurong Island, Singapore Night Race and the Youth Olympics among others.

Mr Chua was a recipient of the Public Administrative Medal (Gold) in 2005 and was awarded the International Management Action Award (MAA) presented by Chartered Management Institute (CMI) Singapore and SPRING Singapore in 2002 for having demonstrated exceptional ability in taking management action to achieve sustainable, tangible results in the rehabilitation of offenders.